A Framework for Teaching Music Online

Also Available from Bloomsbury

The Bloomsbury Handbook of Popular Music Education,
edited by Zack Moir, Bryan Powell, and Gareth Dylan Smith
Education, Music, and the Lives of Undergraduates,
Roger Mantie and Brent C. Talbot
Mastering Primary Music, *Ruth Atkinson*
Music Education with Digital Technology, *edited by John Finney*
The Origins and Foundations of Music Education, 2nd edition,
edited by Gordon Cox and Robin Stevens
Activating Diverse Musical Creativities,
edited by Pamela Burnard and Elizabeth Haddon

A Framework for Teaching Music Online

Carol Johnson

BLOOMSBURY ACADEMIC
LONDON • NEW YORK • OXFORD • NEW DELHI • SYDNEY

BLOOMSBURY ACADEMIC
Bloomsbury Publishing Plc
50 Bedford Square, London, WC1B 3DP, UK
1385 Broadway, New York, NY 10018, USA
29 Earlsfort Terrace, Dublin 2, Ireland

BLOOMSBURY, BLOOMSBURY ACADEMIC and the Diana logo are trademarks of Bloomsbury Publishing Plc

First published in Great Britain 2022
Paperback edition published 2024

Copyright © Carol Johnson, 2022

Carol Johnson has asserted her right under the Copyright, Designs and Patents Act, 1988, to be identified as Author of this work.

For legal purposes the Acknowledgements on p. xiii constitute an extension of this copyright page.

Cover design: Charlotte James
Cover image © valentinrussanov/ Getty Images

All rights reserved. No part of this publication may be reproduced or transmitted in any form or by any means, electronic or mechanical, including photocopying, recording, or any information storage or retrieval system, without prior permission in writing from the publishers.

Bloomsbury Publishing Plc does not have any control over, or responsibility for, any third-party websites referred to or in this book. All internet addresses given in this book were correct at the time of going to press. The author and publisher regret any inconvenience caused if addresses have changed or sites have ceased to exist, but can accept no responsibility for any such changes.

A catalogue record for this book is available from the British Library.

A catalog record for this book is available from the Library of Congress.

ISBN:	HB:	978-1-3502-0186-6
	PB:	978-1-3502-0189-7
	ePDF:	978-1-3502-0185-9
	eBook:	978-1-3502-0187-3

Typeset by Integra Software Services Pvt. Ltd.

To find out more about our authors and books visit www.bloomsbury.com

To my mom

Contents

List of Figures	viii
List of Tables	ix
Preface	x
Foreword	xii
Acknowledgements	xiii
Abbreviations	xiv
Introduction	1

Part 1 Exploring the Framework

1	Presenting the Framework	15
2	Communication	33
3	Communication: Case Studies	45
4	Design	57
5	Design: Case Studies	73
6	Assessment	87
7	Assessment: Case Studies	107

Part 2 Practical Application

8	Considerations for Teaching Music Online	119
9	Designing Your Online Teaching Space	131
10	Selecting Technology Tools and Approaches as Supportive Learning Mechanisms	147

Part 3 Future Innovations

11	Sharing Our Knowledge	159
12	Creating Professional Learning Networks	169

Glossary	178
References	180
Index	195

Figures

1	Continuum of e-Learning	20
2	Detailed Framework for Teaching Music Online: Communication, Design, and Assessment Supported on the Foundations of One's Teaching Philosophy	29
3	Key Considerations of Communication in the Framework for Teaching Music Online	37
4	The Increase of Student Engagement through Considered Online Course Design	60
5	Key Considerations of Design in the Framework for Teaching Music Online	64
6	Assessment Component of Framework for Teaching Music Online	88
7	Creating Student Motivation through Assessment Design Using Feedback and Learner Autonomy	97
8	Scaffolding of Projects to a Final Project	98
9	Comparison of Students' Perceptions Regarding Online Course Cohesion	111
10	Basic Framework for Teaching Music Online	121
11	Dual-Mode Teaching Set-Up	140
12	Weekly Content Folder Organization	142
13	Assessment Folder Organization	142
14	Stepped-LMS Document/Folder Organization	142
15	Establishing Online Presence	155
16	Synchronous Music Activities in Dual-Mode Teaching	164
17	Asynchronous Ensemble Recording Activity Using SoundTrap	165

Tables

1	Examples of Individual and Group Online Assessment Activities	96
2	Example of a Graphic Organizer to Identify Connection of Technology Tools to Class Learning Objectives	150
3	Scholars Writing on the Topic of Online Music Teaching According to Country	175

Preface

We all have a story as to how we came to teaching music online. The brief summary of my introduction to teaching music online came out of my extensive travel to teach musicians in various countries across Latin America back in 2004. Using the minimal technology that was available, and no budget, we started teaching via synchronous text messages. It may sound ridiculous to many, but it was what was available at the time. I tell you this story as it is deeply embedded into *why* I teach music online. Music education access for all, regardless of location, is central to why I have explored how to teach online. This exploration has been a step-by-step process. Each step has revealed new ideas and teaching approaches to consider.

Forging new ways to teach music may be messy at times. New frontiers can be challenging – yet they are not unsurmountable. We move forward one step at a time – *paso a paso* – whether we are on a gentle footpath or traversing a mountain crag. No journey is impossible when we believe in the goal.

The journey of teaching music online is complex; there is much to consider and transform in this new teaching approach. Teaching music, online learning, creativity, resilience, and artistic performance are just a small surface list of considerations as we seek effective online teaching practices.

It is not expected that an entire conservatorium or school move all music courses online. However, those engaged in teaching music in the twenty-first century should evidence effective technology adoption for the purposes of inclusive education (e.g., Universal Design for Learning opportunities of video, text, and audio), curriculum differentiation (e.g., addressing student-based learning needs), and musically supportive assessment and feedback mechanisms. While not a cure for bad teaching, online music courses that are well-designed can help students develop self-regulation skills and overcome some of the challenges of well-being and mental health that are reported across the university disciplines. Finally, the challenges of risk management and disaster planning/recovery – a notable issue in the 2020 Coronavirus outbreak – can be further mitigated through online course offerings when carefully designed and strategically implemented.

The outcome of a framework for teaching music online is found in its implementation – we have to read about it, examine it, and then try it out before we can personalize it for our specific teaching needs. May these pages be trusted companions of encouragement and support wherever you are at along your online music teaching journey.

Foreword

The ever-changing world of music education relies on leaders who can shape our thinking and help redefine past practices. This is especially important for the area of online learning and educational technologies where events such as the Covid-19 pandemic and rapid developments in technology demand we evolve our teaching to accommodate the multitude of ways that individuals of all ages engage in and interact with music. And so it was with the greatest pleasure that I opened my copy of *Framework for Teaching Online* to read explanations of how the three macro elements of design, communication, and assessment can stimulate a reconceptualization of how to teach music online. What I enjoyed most about this publication was learning about the multiple ways to explore teaching from an evidence-based perspective, and the highly practical and how-to suggestions from which to guide our work. Carol Johnson's *Framework for Teaching Online* will serve seasoned music teachers through to those who are just commencing in the profession. The overarching message presented by its author is the unique opportunity to create a global learning community in which we can all be learners, share ideas, and mentor each other. These are worthy ideals for a publication that will surely inspire a generation of music educators.

Gary McPherson
Ormond Professor of Music
The University of Melbourne, Australia

Acknowledgements

Many thanks to the many people that have helped support making this book into a reality. Specifically, I wish to thank my family (Mom, Dad, Linda, Scott, Mac, Bren, AV, and the Johnson crew) who have provided tireless encouragement across the years, and friends (BB, CH, MH, AH, CD, and KM) who have sent an extra prayer my way. You all had a part in this.

Thank you to BL and TC for their work in editing.

Many thanks to the wonderful team at Bloomsbury, with special thanks to Alison, who have made this work a reality.

Thanks to the University of Melbourne, Conservatorium of Music, for supporting innovations in teaching music online. A research grant was received which helped support this book.

Abbreviations

AUS	Australia
CAN	Canada
COI	Community of Inquiry framework
F2F	Face-to-face
LMS	Learning Management System
OL	Online Learning
OMP	Online Music Pedagogy
US	United States of America

Introduction

Early records, such as Plato's Republic, herald the importance of music teaching for the individual and society. Described as a 'more potent instrument than any other' (Plato, 1970, p. 401), music teaching, and more broadly the making and experiencing of music, is a unique aspect of who we are as humans. As we progress through the timeline of music teaching history, we can observe key shifts, innovations, and seasons of change experienced by those who teach music and its students.

The quest to continue the heritage of music teaching, and therefore musiking, is a key point for cultures and society as a whole (Mark & Gary, 2007). It is therefore from this place of purpose that this book is set out not only to highlight an approach to teaching music, but to preserve the legacy of music teaching for another generation, or possibly even another generation yet to come.

To provide a well-supported structure of information about the online music framework and its connections to music education, and education overall, the book is divided into three inter-connected sections. The first section of the book (Chapter 1 to Chapter 7) outlines the need for a framework, and then explains the three components of the framework with case studies as examples in practice. Building upon the structured framework, the book's second section (Chapter 8 to Chapter 10) focuses on practical ways music teachers can innovate their online music classes by way of purposeful classroom design and technology tool selection. To provide a sustainable future in enhancing one's online music teaching, the final section (Chapter 11 and Chapter 12) explores opportunities for innovation and knowledge sharing through the continued momentum of oneself as lifelong music learner.

Why Online Music Teaching?

As teachers, it is important to know *why* we choose to teach music, and why we choose to implement specific teaching strategies and approaches. Reflecting on why we teach and why we select a specific teaching approach over another can provide insights into improving our overall teaching practice. It is also important to note that in the area of music, music teachers in higher education often find themselves teaching music without having a teaching degree (Mitchell, 2020a) and 83 per cent of music academics suggest their music students will find themselves becoming music teachers after graduation (Fredrickson et al., 2013).

Appreciating that music teachers have spent more time honing their musicianship skills, it is understood that no matter how we find ourselves placed in music teaching, awareness of research-informed music teaching practices can be beneficial.

Research-informed teaching practices can be niche music teaching strategies, as well as practices that are formed from broader teaching and learning theories. When we consider the area of teaching music online, we bring together both research-informed practices that are specific to music teaching and music education in general, as well as the larger scope of online learning and general learning theory. These practices come together in an area first termed 'online music pedagogy' by Fernanda Oliveira-Torres (2012). Online music pedagogy (OMP) is described as 'the pedagogical aspects influencing course development and learning outcomes in online music courses' (Johnson, 2017, p. 442). While the specificities of OMP are continuing to be made explicit, it is established that this form of teaching is informed by music education, online learning, and education practices.

Bringing together diverse fields of teaching and learning allows the opportunity to use teaching practices that have shown effective research-based student learning outcomes while addressing a particular discipline in terms of authenticity. Authenticity is not a new term in any teaching field; authenticity is part of what we teach, and how we teach. It is directly linked to the actual real-world discipline of music itself. With authenticity in our teaching, students experience the real-world discipline in a learning environment that should allow students to explore, investigate, and practise the discipline within a 'safety net' environment. For example, as musicians, musical authenticity typically references the acknowledgement and use of specific historical performance practices, musical styles, or musical sounds and instruments.

When thinking of authenticity in terms of teaching music online, there is a need to effectively thread together the student learning experience, learning content and approach, as well as teaching approach (e.g., teaching strategies, assessments, approaches to feedback) across the entire learning experience (see Chapter 6). From this perspective, authenticity becomes a term that we can use to help us navigate the decisions we make to select what activities and approaches are most suited for teaching music online.

Evaluating teaching authenticity can be a tenuous path as our individual beliefs and values of music (e.g., music as art; music as experience), and how to teach music, shift to a more visible position. How we teach is often a display of our beliefs in action. When we take time to explore our own beliefs and values of teaching, it can better support those areas that are unfamiliar. Self-reflection on our own teaching beliefs can provide insight and opportunities for exploration of how we can teach more effectively in our music classrooms – regardless of the teaching medium.

The Historical Journey of Online Music Learning

As we seek to understand online music learning, it's important to consider how the field of teaching has been strongly influenced and impacted by other disciplines. As such, this section will take the opportunity to explore online learning and its development across the past decades and its influence in contemporary learning practices and teaching approaches.

Moore and Kearsley (2011) detail the historical background of how distance learning evolved and its relationship of learning across location and time. If we think back to the use of mail service for correspondence lessons, we can easily understand that distance learning has occurred for a couple hundred years. This extensive history of learning is differentiated by Kaufman (1989) into the use of print and broadcasting technologies (i.e., mono-directional technologies) and telephony (i.e., bidirectional technologies). Multiple approaches and multiple tools dot the timeline of distance learning history. The evolutionary thread visible throughout the various descriptions of distance learning is its inclusion of technology – an aspect that is central to the definition of online learning.

There are many different ways to approach the history of online learning. Some choose to navigate its history through the focus of technology usage. It is from this viewpoint that Kaufman (1989) suggests three movements have taken place in distance learning: the use of mono-directional technologies (e.g., print and broadcasting technologies), the use of bidirectional technologies (e.g., telephony), and a mixture of non-synchronous formats. With the 1993 unveiling of the internet to the public, we had a 'soft launch' of online learning. Learning exchanges through university intranets, basic text email, and Archie searches became possible for the innovator from the late 1990s within higher education context (Picciano, 2006). Together, these avenues of distance learning influenced the evolution of technology-enhanced learning that we experience in the twenty-first century.

Technology use in our learning can be a love-hate relationship. It seems to welcome a vocabulary of terms that are often in flux. Similarly, as instructors, we continue to evolve our technology tools according to our personal views, our students' use, and our institution's learning culture (Johnson, 2018a). Many scholars have discussed outcomes that have occurred from the adoption of technology-enhanced learning approaches in general academia (see Spector, 2001; Wang & Hannafin, 2005) as well as in music (see Peters, 1992; Waddell & Williamon, 2019; Webster, 2007). There have been many challenges and adjustments along this historical journey and adoption of online teaching technologies has taken place over multiple decades.

The 2000s: Fully Online Classes

There will always be outliers to a generalized timeline of technology diffusion (see Rogers, 2003). Location, social context, and economic privilege have played problematic roles in an equitable offering of internet and opportunity for anyone to take part. However, there is an overarching sequence of adoption as evidenced in the writing of Power (2020).

Providing an in-depth historical survey of distance learning approaches used in Canadian universities, Michael Power (2020) details how universities have integrated the use of text and voice in educational technologies to support learning in undergraduate and graduate students. In his opening chapter of *The Finest Blend* (2020), Power suggests that the incorporation of text and voice can be visualized in terms of swings of a pendulum. While the initial pendulum action started with the inclusion of text in distance education (e.g., correspondence classes), Power suggests it swung back and forth for four more 'generations' (p. 23), which resulted in the emergence of online learning in the 1990s. Picciano (2006) previously outlined notable stages of transitions when he wrote his own clarion call for higher education institutions to effectively prepare for online learning through the adoption of supportive policies for personnel, infrastructure, and technical support.

Notably, during this time, the online class was becoming its own unique learning space—a space that required a different approach than a face-to-face classroom (Redmon, 2011). This was very evident for the innovators of the online music class as reported by Finnish music researchers who were already publishing on the essential teaching tools for online music education in the late 1990s and early 2000s (Ruippo, 1999, 2003). Other international innovators such as McGill University (CA), Manhattan School of Music (USA), and

Royal College of Music (UK) were also looking at ways to make their music classes accessible to larger audiences through the online environment (Lisboa et al., 2022). Yet, the cost of expensive technologies often made online music learning prohibitive for small universities, as well as individuals, to take part.

The ebb and flow of technology changes, costs, and perceptions continued to impact the adoption of online learning in universities. Power (2020) recognizes the noted pull away from online as his descriptive pendulum swung again with the invariable shift, but this time to a blended learning model that appeared in mid-2000s. From Power's descriptive historical text, we can see that the 'tick-tock' pendulum changed according to the degree to which technology was embraced in teaching. There was a push and pull which came from differing responses by administration, instructors, and students. Power (2020) further suggests that the disruptive change was closely linked to aspects of 'content volatility' (p. 27), intricate balance of pro-campus and innovators, as well as 'purportedly' (p. 29) supporting minimal disruption for teacher workload.

As we think back to the late-2000s, we are reminded of the appearance of the smart phone. A small device, but with a big financial impact: supply and demand. Further decreased technology costs took place due to the increased demand for computers and internet in homes. This meant more access to technology for the public user than ever before.

While businesses had been the driver for most computer-aided technology up to the 2000s, the global demand for computing technology in the public sector provided a tipping point for technological advancement. Some of us can recall this time vividly. Perhaps you were an 'innovator' or 'early adopter' (see Rogers, 2003) and found yourself as owner of one of the first iPhones that came to market in January 2007. This technology tool's popularity signalled further business opportunities within mobile – and internet – technology. Internet-connected computers in every home became a closer reality for many. However, the inherent 'digital divide' (Hill & Lawton, 2018) in conjunction with online learning further enforced the gap between which students could afford to take online courses.

The 2010s: Positioning of Effective Online Instruction

It is important to highlight that during this time period of online learning, many universities are already exploring the advantages of online learning within the academic STEM (Science, Technology, Engineering, and Mathematics) disciplines. Practice-based and lab-dependent disciplines were not yet common in the online environment, although there were innovators exploring the possibilities (Mayadas et al., 2009). It was also during this timeframe that Jeffrey Allen and Elaine Seaman begin surveying universities across the United States regarding the adoption rate of online classes. Their annual reports became seminal publications that detail the acceptance of online learning over years (see Allen & Seaman, 2013).

Moving into the early 2010s, it became evident that the lower cost of video conferencing technology meant that instructors could create their own videos without the expensive use of institutional audio-visual teams. Many academic instructors found themselves not only teaching online, but taking up the role of online instructional designers as more classes were offered online. This meant instructors had further opportunity to edit their own videos with more voice in decision-making for online and blended course content. While not every instructor had skills in video production and online instructional design, those keen to take up key technology skills found themselves with the ability to create basic online classes using graphics, videos, and animated gifs.

We learned a lot in the early years of designing online content. If you were teaching at that time, you may recall seeing text-heavy content pages or even the occasional cute, animated guinea pig gifs scattered across a web page. During this time, the research of Meyer and other colleagues (see Meyer & Moreno, 2003) surfaced the importance to carefully consider inclusion of multimedia so that learners do not experience cognitive overload. Simply put, research gave us helpful insight into practical instructional design guidelines. Effective use of multimedia in online learning meant that the images related to the learning content and that distracting page design (e.g., font, page layout) wasn't conducive for effective learning. Instructors faced a large learning curve with additional workload of learning how to use new technologies and their best practices. It is understandable how the online instructional design degree became a commodity to have in the education sector at this time.

Building on established learning theories, instructional design models and theories further advanced how the use of technology can support learning (Branch & Kopcha, 2014). At the same time, the focus towards student-centred learning became firmly established in teaching models for higher education (Wright, 2011). Combined with online learning's double-digit adoption rate in Higher Education (Allen & Seaman, 2013), online learning in the mid-2010s was becoming an approach that could address differentiated learning approaches through careful instructional design and educational learning theory.

As the online class became more common in higher education, researchers explored students' perceptions and personal experiences in online learning (Macon, 2011). Studies highlighted the similarities and differences of student learning experiences within online classes. Meta-analyses further evidenced how online classes were equivalent to their face-to-face counterparts for students in academic disciplines in higher education (Bowen et al., 2013; Means et al., 2009).

By the early-to-mid 2010s, online music instruction was becoming more popular and increased in availability across universities. For example, the National Association of Schools of Music (NASM)-accredited universities in the United States are reported as offering Bachelor-level online music classes at an exponential rate of increase starting in 2012 (Johnson, 2021). Furthermore, research in networked music performances were being explored between Milan, Italy, and Copenhagen, Denmark (Delle Monache et al., 2019), with the Connect ReSound project in England (King et al., 2019).

A blended teaching approach provided instructors with opportunities to post relevant videos for students to view and review, in addition to archiving additional reading resources, YouTube video links, and relevant website links. This cornucopia of resource options often resulted in the development of the 'class and a half syndrome' wherein instructors create an online class that contains rich resources and teaching content beyond the time limitations allocated for class completion.

As found in any technological disruption, change is a necessary element (Rogers, 2003). A new technology tool emerges, and one is inclined to examine if, and to what degree, it is helpful for student learning. Face-to-face, online, and blended learning has appeared to be terms that are now commonplace across universities and schools. Yet, each of these terms continues to evolve in their own unique way.

However, the prioritization and overall debate for how to choose between online learning, blended learning, and face-to-face classes continue as universities cater to their specific student demographics and unique institutional culture. A blend of these approaches were often offered to students. The refinement of these approaches also came with new names (e.g., Technology-Enhanced Learning (TEL); HiFlex learning) and further adoption of technologies. Terms common to technology-enhanced learning included: web-based learning (Keller, 2005), blended online learning (Power, 2008), hybrid and blended learning (Means et al., 2009), synchronous learning, and blended-synchronous learning (Bower et al., 2015).

As we approached 2020, students typically graduated with more than one online class in their Bachelor's degree (Seaman et al., 2018). Unknown to all, the 'more than one' online class statistic was about to drastically change.

The 2020s: Ready for Anything

As we reflect on the start of the 2020s, we have likely experienced a lifetime of teaching discomfort and challenge in a very short time frame. The 2020 Covid-19 pandemic has impacted our social communities, travel, and education experiences – and tragically resulted in the devastating loss of lives.

Unquestionably, students in practice-based classes, like music, were affected given the overnight transition to online classes (Ritchie & Sharpe, 2021). Classes that had already started their technological transformation were also affected. However, it would be reasonable to suggest that instructors teaching in a F2F traditional paradigm of music – and the arts, in general – felt an acutely abrupt teaching transition.

It is from this historical context that we begin our individual online music teaching journey. As musicians, we have studied to be improvisors and creatives; as instructors, we now can re-create and re-define the music classroom for the future.

Teaching Music Online

Teaching music online can be designed to support students through flexibility, equity, and accessibility. These key mechanisms are not unique to online music classes. In combination, they are viewed as beneficial outcomes for those inquiring about the validity of online music learning.

The flexible nature of taking an online class allows for students to continue working while studying and attending to carer responsibilities. For example, an online student may be responsible for childcare during the day and choose to complete an online course during hours that are more convenient than a Monday to Friday on-campus class.

An often-understated consideration for online learning is the affordance of accessibility through the supportive nature of asynchronous learning. That is, some may want to revisit learning content for remedial or extended learning.

When carefully constructed, online learning can support equity of student learning. That is, students are able to learn through the inclusion of multimedia, have opportunity to access learning in an individualized manner, and evidence their learning in various formats. Together, this concept addresses aspects of Universal Design for Learning (Meyer et al., 2014) that will be further explored in Chapter 1.

Online learning further supports student accessibility through the opportunity to design learning experiences that include both asynchronous and synchronous activities. The option of being able to access the learning content 24/7 and participate in asynchronous learning activities can be a motivation for students who are not able to be on-campus during regular business hours due to their geographic location – both rural and urban. The inclusion of online synchronous activities also allows learners to engage in real-time conversations, workshops, and discussions that may not physically be possible. (This format became popularized as a response to pandemic lockdowns in various countries in 2020.) The requirement to be on-campus for real-time events has been challenged as a result of the pandemic teaching experience. Online synchronous activities became a normalized teaching format. Since this technological disruption, more students are now able to experience music learning across their cities, states, and countries in an unprecedented manner. It suggests that perhaps one's proximity to campus may no longer be a prohibitive factor to completing a degree on campus, or within a particular country. The discussion of boundary of place (e.g., commute to campus, or global location) and its connected housing and travel costs is more prevalent in conversations as online music learning takes deeper root across universities and colleges.

This shift of place in learning does not have to equate with a loss of university culture and student experience. Again, with a careful and considered approach, framing the learning of music online can provide learners with unique learning outcomes moored in hallmarks aligned with each institution.

Misconceptions of Learning Music Online at a Postsecondary Level

Assumptions and misconceptions abound regarding learning music online: Is learning online effective? What can be taught online – and what can't? Our response to each of these questions can be different based on the assumptions, as well as misconceptions, we hold.

It is important to be aware that we have assumptions, as well as misconceptions, on various topics, ideals, and approaches in teaching. An assumption may stop us from trying something new, or perhaps it may keep us doing the same thing.

In teaching music online, there are some key assumptions and misconceptions that we, and those around us, may have yet to examine and/or overcome. Let's take a moment to examine what assumptions we may hold regarding teaching music online.

Use the following questions to surface assumptions about teaching music online. Take time to include a few reasons for each particular response.

1. Online students receive a less-rigorous learning experience than face-to-face students.
2. Learning online and learning face-to-face are similar teaching approaches.
3. Face-to-face music teaching provides all students with the best learning experience.
4. Music is a creative experience that cannot be expressed online.
5. Teaching music online is more difficult than teaching face-to-face.

It is important to briefly address each of these statements to help surface assumptions we may have about teaching music online. I encourage you to come back to the statements once you finish reading this book and explore your responses again.

Misconception 1: Online students receive a less-rigorous learning experience than face-to-face students

This statement is based on a presumption that online learning isn't rigorous. However, one could argue that face-to-face classes are not rigorous. What makes a class (online or face-to-face) rigorous? It is reasonable to suggest that the careful crafting of class design and transparent expectations of the learning and assessment experience strongly support a rigorous learning outcome.

Misconception 2: Learning online and learning face-to-face are similar teaching approaches

This statement suggests that all learning, and therefore how we approach every learner is the same. However, we know that students are unique and individual learners. Furthermore, this statement would suggest that the approaches used in the online environment would work as well in the face-to-face environment, and the approaches of a face-to-face classroom work in an online classroom. However, the first requirement of online learning is the use of technology to access the learning – no technology, no access to online learning. This foundational requirement opens a larger dialogue of the unique aspects to online and face-to-face teaching. Briefly consider the differences of teaching a class on sand versus teaching a class in the water. Teaching and learning is occurring, but there are different approaches that need to be considered so that everyone has a successful (and safe!) learning experience. There are some similar tools used, but the approaches to teaching are set up unique for the environment. We set up our pedagogical paradigms for the learning mediums we will be using – and we should look to use effective teaching approaches specific to the teaching medium.

Misconception 3: Face-to-face music teaching provides all students with the best learning experience

The unveiling of the internet in the 1990s opened the door to exploring the affordances of teaching online. Discussion on what types of music classes can, and should, be taught fully online, is a continued point of debate and comes with a broad spectrum of opinions. Researchers continue to investigate questions that explore many questions that include *what specific music disciplines can be taught effectively online?*, as well as questions like *to what extent, and how, music activities can effectively take place in the online class?* (Forsyth et al., 2013; Hebert, 2007; Johnson, 2021; Koutsoupidou, 2014; Lisboa et al., 2022). Within this field of research, perhaps another question we should be asking is: What students are choosing to learning music online and why? We know that online learning is not for everyone, but similarly, face-to-face learning isn't either. So, we have some research work to explore to better understand the extent to which effective music learning happens in both environments.

Misconception 4: Music is a creative experience that cannot be expressed online

Perhaps this statement is short-sighted with regard to the definition of creativity and music. We would need to tease out more about this misconception. Is it that music has to take place live and synchronous to warrant a creative experience? If so, then how do we position the twentieth century's acceptance to the use of taped music with regard to creative experience? Or, would we classify singers taking part in an online synchronous choir lacking a creative experience while they sing?

There are many opportunities surrounding the creative music experience and technology. The online environment has opened up doors to new expressions of music composition (e.g., Networked Music Performances; Latency Tolerant Music Composition). Perhaps the question is more ontological and personal in exploration in that it requires us to define music and creativity. The unique intricacies of musical expression have found itself navigating across the millennia and taking up new approaches to music making and using technologies. Subsequently, the online environment is just one more medium for us to consider in our creative process.

Misconception 5: Teaching music online is more difficult than teaching face-to-face

Great teaching is a lot of work no matter the place or space. So, let's get started in learning how to create great online learning!

Part One

Exploring the Framework

The initial chapter in this section presents the Framework for Teaching Music Online with the three components illustrated in its complete iterative cycle. Examples of how to move through the entire cycle are provided. The rest of Part One explores framework components individually (i.e., Communication, Design and Assessment) and concludes with the framework in its full construction. The summation of each component chapter includes examples of how the component could be implemented and is followed by a case study chapter evidencing the component. Each case research narrative evidences how the component is a key developmental concept for teaching music online.

1

Presenting the Framework

Introduction

Teaching music in the online environment is not merely about using technology and technology tools in one's teaching. Teaching music online is founded upon the blending of essential teaching practices from the fields of education, online learning, and music education. The blending of these pedagogical practices is not an exact science but an art. And supporting the learning and performance needs of the music student remains the focus of teaching music online. However, given the nascent field of online music pedagogy, there is a need to explore how and what components support music performance learning. This chapter aims to outline the need for a framework in teaching music online.

Locating the place on the timeline of history to start the discussion on teaching and learning can be challenging. There are many eminent scholars, theories, and seminal works that form our ideas today on understanding how we learn. Knowing how we learn positions us for ensuring our teaching can effectively support our students.

Theory of Constructivism

It's helpful to have a solid mooring to learning theory when we are exploring new approaches to teaching. Learning theory helps us to better understand how we learn and places us in a posture for more effective design and delivery of our teaching.

As we look back on the twentieth century, one of the significant scholars exploring the research of learning was John Dewey (1938). His early twentieth-century work, while understated at the time, examined the importance of reflection in learning. Dewey (1910) stated, 'We reflect in order that we may get hold of the full and adequate significance of what happens. Nevertheless, something must be already understood, the mind must be in possession of some meaning which it is mastered, or else thinking is impossible' (p. 120). This notion of each learner having acquired knowledge and building up on that knowledge through critical thinking and reflection refers to the theory of constructivism. In brief, this complex theory suggests that as learners, we use our previous experiences and activities to inform and construct our current knowledge and understanding.

Furthering our understanding on the importance of learning through our actions, Jean Piaget examined cognition, learner as active participant, and the development stages of learning in children (Winzer, 1992). While controversy surrounds his ethical research practices, his findings surfaced impacts and influences of consequential outcomes of learners on their world and on those around them. Focused on the process of how individuals learn, Piaget identified important formations, such as social transmission, that would pave the way to later learning theory researchers, such as Bandura (1981) and Vygotsky (1978), and the theory of social constructivism.

The importance of how we create meaning from our learned experiences cannot be underscored. Understanding the process of learning, how we construct our learning, and the importance of social experiences in learning, positions instructors to be well placed in the design of meaningful learning for students. It is from this point that it can be understood why the use of teaching approaches such as student-centred learning (Jonassen, 1992), problem-based learning (Jonassen, 2013; Merrill, 2002), and sequential learning (Wiggins & McTige, 2005), inherently sets students up for learning success.

The research folio of Jonassen crosses many decades from the 1990s to 2010s. His work identified many key aspects for effective student learning when using technology. In his early research (1995) he highlighted the importance of 'authenticity' (p. 21) as it relates to the incorporation of educational technology into teaching. (Note: The specific approach of authenticity is further explored in the framework itself in *Chapter 6* on authentic assessment.) The study also surfaced how technology use can become opportunities for increased student interaction in their learning. Specifically, educational technologies provided a significant paradigm shift for how students engage in learning. Data from the study identified that the teacher involvement decreased from 80 per cent down to 10–15 per cent when students were given opportunity to have more direct interaction with their learning. That is, when technology was used to help support students' autonomy in learning, they were able to have a more individualized learning experience. It may seem obvious that students have more focused learning time when using technology; you may even have the image of a student staring into a computer screen. However, it is important to bring to the forefront that instead of the previous 80 per cent teacher-led class, classes using technology (albeit carefully planned activities that are supported by technology tools) can result in student-centred learning. Student centred learning is an important outcome as it is connected to student motivation and supportive self-regulation skills (Hattie, 2012). The inclusion of educational technology further focused allocated time for students to be engaged as active learners (e.g., through mental, physical, and effective aspects in learning).

Jonassen's lifetime of scholarship in the area of student learning unveils many complexities of learning to reveal important considerations for creating effective learning experiences for students. These experiences focus on providing students with opportunities to examine their current knowledge through reflection, create informed decisions from their examination, and then act upon decisions in a personal and meaningful way. Together with the large corpus of the literature on learning theory, we see that effective teaching practices provide students with opportunities to self-reflect, make informed decisions, and use those decisions through means of active learning experiences to solidify a deep learning experience (Biggs, 1987).

While we can create learning experiences that are meant to activate student learning for key skills and knowledge attainment, it is important to keep in mind that every student is unique; therefore, a unique learning outcome should be anticipated. This, however, does not mean that broad learning objectives are not achieved. It suggests that there is opportunity for students to achieve different levels of learning outcomes. To this degree, it is important that students have the opportunity to evidence and demonstrate their learning across diverse representation to successfully '*show what they know*'.

Universal Design for Learning

Universal Design for Learning (UDL) (see Meyer et al., 2014) is a key approach for ensuring diversity of learning. This framework consists of 'a set of principles for curriculum development that gives all individuals equal opportunities to learn' (National Centre on Universal Design for Learning, 2014, para. 1).

As we explore the inclusion of UDL in learning, it becomes obvious that technology plays a role. Findings from various research studies support the positive outcomes of technology use in higher education. With approximately 25 per cent of today's adults described as 'almost constantly online' (Perrin & Jiang, 2018) with 40 per cent of online adult learners spending three to four hours each day working online (EDUCAUSE, 2018), it is understandable that using technology for learning is a regular part of student's lives. Perhaps unsurprisingly, many students have positive attitudes towards using technology in their studies. For example, the quantitative research involving 292 higher education students by Lai, Wang, and Lei (2012) showed that less than 2 per cent of students did not have internet access and their overall positive perceptions of technology led students to voluntarily use technology to support their learning. From this, it can be suggested that students are willing to embrace technology in their learning. While technology can provide students with student-centred and meaningful learning opportunities, there is a need to consider the ways to approach effective teaching with technology.

In her work on designing tertiary online learning environments, Altowairiki (2016) explores the effectiveness of UDL instructional design in higher education classes. The findings suggest that the three UDL principles of Meyer et al. (2014) – i.e., multiple means of engagement, multiple means of action in expression, and multiple means of representation – are an effective framework for designing and supporting students' learning online in higher education. Importantly, the inherent building and designing of learning content – with considered attention with regard to how multiple forms of multimedia (i.e., video, audio, and text) are placed – can help ensure inclusive learning pathways for all students. Combined with the design and implementation research of multimedia by Clark and Mayer (2003, 2008), learners can experience an online course without the challenge and distraction of increased cognitive load.

Essentials of Teaching

Irrespective of the discipline, scholars have identified that there are critical components for effective teaching. In 1987, Chickering and Gamson highlighted seven critical elements for undergraduate teaching. These elements were: contact between students, reciprocity, active learning, prompt feedback, time on task, communication of expectations, and diversity of learning approaches. When we look at the specific teaching elements, it is likely that there is no surprise in the listing. Furthermore, when we re-examine these seven elements through the lens of developing approaches for student engagement, we might find ourselves compiling these elements into a checklist to help create and evaluate our learning environment to better support the inspiration and motivation for sustained student participation in our own classes.

As education has become more integrated with technology, updates have been made to these principles (Chickering & Erhmann, 1996) in addition to instructional design approaches for online learning (Bigatel et al., 2012). The writing of Garrison (2011) further highlights online learning essentials to consider when teaching as well as a need for a pedagogical shift to occur among faculty members moving from traditional teaching environments to online environment as a result of increased technology use.

Defining Online Learning

In his research in online learning, Garrison (2011) suggests that the overarching term e-learning can bring together the broad descriptions of blended and online learning. This definition surfaces the key aspect of digital technology use (see Figure 1). But to surface the nuanced differences of these two approaches to learning, it is helpful to consider a 'continuum of technology-based learning' (Bates, 2015, p. 366). With face-to-face learning and online learning as the end posts of the continuum, it becomes more obvious as to the fluidity of some terms, such as blended learning.

To further aid clarity to the terms often used in teaching, it is helpful to understand the detailed nuances of these terms. *Face-to-face* (F2F) learning is used to describe the type of learning that occurs when 29 per cent or less of the teaching and content is located online (Allen & Seaman, 2014). In their extensive analysis of data across the years, Allen and Seaman describe the other end of the continuum as online learning when 80 per cent or more of its teaching and content is located online. Together, this creates a more definitive understanding of how to consider the broad approach of blended learning – a term that is increasingly common in today's twenty-first-century learning climate.

Comprising a mix of both F2F and online learning, blended learning forms a varied composite (see Garrison, 2011; Means et al., 2010). While there are

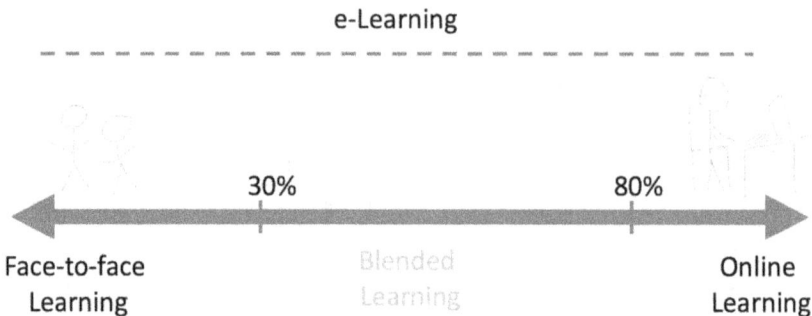

Figure 1 Continuum of e-Learning.

small differences within each of these terms, they basically identify that students experience a limited form of live on-campus classes, or live-streamed classes in combination with the majority of their class using online platforms for teaching and learning. It is noted that dual-mode teaching does not fit seamlessly into the blended learning category as it has two approaches to learning – online and on-campus learning – happening synchronously at the same time. The blending of learning approaches requires more planning and design than a single teaching approach. See Chapter 9 for practical approaches for dual mode teaching in music.

For over ten years, researchers Jeff Allen and Elaine Seaman reported on the historical development of online classes in higher education across the United States. Starting with an initial report in 2002 (see Allen & Seaman, 2004), their research evidences the acceptance of online course offerings. Their reports also give insight into the perceptions of administration and academic faculty members regarding the use of online learning and their resulting learning outcomes across the years. These reports show that negative perceptions have decreased significantly since their initial reports and give support for the need for faculty professional development when transitioning to online teaching.

In his writing furthering the understanding of e-learning, and the Community of Inquiry model, Garrison (2011) stated, 'The challenge is to understand the emerging education environment and how we create and sustain communities of inquiry that will facilitate the development of higher-order learning' (p. 18). While Garrison's work is focused on the broad overlay of e-learning across higher education, studies of online music instruction by Dye (2007) and Eakes (2009) also elucidate key pedagogical challenges (e.g., technology tools and approaches to course design) when transitioning from F2F to the online teaching environment and confirm the need for online music pedagogy in online music courses. From these early studies, and others, we understand that there are key teaching essentials that need to be put in place when teaching music online.

Essentials for Teaching Music Online

In education, we can see accessibility addressed through the progressive inclusion of online learning as over 6.7 students have taken at least one online course by their last year of Bachelor study (Allen & Seaman, 2013). The relevancy of online learning essentials becomes apparent as well-designed online education courses can demonstrate and identify meaningful constructivist and higher-order learning (Anderson & Krathwohl, 2001; Jonassen, 2013; Vygotsky, 1978) and connected learning presence (Garrison et al., 2001; Picciano, 2002). Comparatively, the use of traditional F2F pedagogy in music education is described as limited in its inclusion of currently available technologies (Allsup & Benedict, 2008; Purves, 2012), even though music education researchers support the inclusion of constructivist learning and new technologies (Purves, 2012; Webster, 2007).

Research confirms the effectiveness of online music education technology (Adileh, 2012; Draper, 2008; Eakes, 2009; Hammond, 2005), community needs of musicians (Salavuo, 2006), and deeper learning and cognitive development (Dye, 2007). This begins to unmask many layers of questions with regard to technology use, and non-use, in higher education music classes. Consequently, one of the purposes of this larger exploration in research, which resulted in the development of the framework outlined in this book, was to identify and define essential connections of current online learning approaches and music education instruction. As a result, the framework itself is a response to the instructional course design, communication technologies, and pedagogy as informed by appropriate research and practice.

Purpose of the Framework

The centrality of musicianship requires a learning environment that creatively affords personalized learning, self-reflection, sustainable community interaction and collaboration, multiple access points for inclusive learning, and scalable teaching. In general, online music education research affords support to the complexities of programme relevance and geographic accessibility by providing a framework to guide the development of effective music education utilizing current technologies. Our contemporary world is now a connected culture through the internet that, through the research of online music pedagogy, can bring together many languages, cultures, and countries with marginalized people to experience social inclusivity and share music creativity.

Teaching higher education music students in a fully online course format was an emerging practice in the early 2010s (Groulx & Hernly, 2010; Johnson, 2021). 'With the ubiquity of online learning, an increased awareness of the need for greater accessibility to music lessons, and a recognition that online music study can fill some of the existing gap, instrumental music teachers need to develop competency in teaching music online' (Pike, forthcoming). The need to teach music online was magnified starting in 2020 as a result of the Covid-19 pandemic.

Faced with decisions to either pause teaching or transition to an online platform, many music instructors were strongly encouraged by university administration to transition their face-to-face music performance and general music classes to the online environment. Preliminary and final research identified an exponentially increasing implementation of online music classes in higher education since 2012 in the United States (Johnson, 2021; Johnson & Hawley, 2017). Other countries, like Australia, had yet to embrace fully online classes in university Bachelor of Music degrees programmes (Johnson & Cheok, in review). While teaching music online is yet to be widely accepted by post-secondary music programmes and conservatoires around the world, a notable number of research projects have investigated explicit components within the area of teaching music online.

In the recently updated *Oxford Handbook of Music Education*, Lisboa et al. (2022) outlined a brief historical timeline of synchronous online music teaching in higher education. Their chapter also documents much of the research specific to online music performance teaching in one place and presents a summation of approaches for using technologies when teaching music online. Citing studies from across the world, it is evident that many researchers and music teachers have been exploring the various music learning opportunities afforded by the online environment prior to 2010.

In the general area of online music learning, researchers have explored: constructivism in online music teaching (Keast, 2009; Scott, 2006), online music lessons (Dye, 2007), effectiveness of online music education technology

(Draper, 2008; Dye, 2007; Eakes, 2009; Hammond, 2005), online learning as supportive of musicians' community needs (Salavuo, 2006), development of deeper music learning and cognitive skills (Dye, 2007), and much more. Together, these topics suggest that when teachers take up these research-informed practices, their students can experience effective music learning in an online environment.

However, online music teaching is not a mere 'lift and shift' of F2F teaching design and F2F activities into an online environment. As outlined above, teaching online is, itself, a unique teaching approach. Therefore, an effective online teaching environment for music requires a pedagogical paradigm shift (Johnson, 2017). Knowledge of, and implementation of key online teaching design approaches and overall, online pedagogical principles and theories, must be considered when teaching music online.

Given the difference in teaching approach in the online environment, it is valid to question as to how such a philosophical change may impact those already teaching music in higher education.

When exploring the research on the backgrounds of academics teaching music in higher education (Mitchell, 2020a), we find that many enter their teaching in a music faculty with a focused expertise in music but with minimal formal study in music education, or teaching, in general. We know that expertise in the discipline of music is paramount – this is not contested. However, given the intricacies developing an online class in general, perhaps we also need to consider how the combination of pedagogical knowledge and music teaching expertise can further influence an optimal transition to teaching music in the online environment. 'Instructional design of online courses is of paramount importance since music learning involves multi-sensory and multiple modalities of learning, in addition to systematic and careful development of complex physical and technical skills' (Pike, forthcoming). Furthermore, research regarding the impact of prior pedagogical knowledge on the transition to online teaching is beginning to surface from the many Covid-19 studies regarding the successes, and challenges, of the overnight shift from F2F to online music teaching due to the 2020 pandemic (see Joseph & Lennox, 2021; Merrick & Johnson, 2021; Schiavio et al., 2021).

One of the overarching challenges identified by music instructors moving to teach online was, and is, the magnitude of change involved. From the current research, findings suggest that not only do students need high levels of self-regulation skills when learning online (Allen & Seaman, 2013), but online music instructors also need to position themselves to be willing to change their teaching practices. Change is also termed as a 'growth mindset' (Dweck, 2016). In short, those with an openness to change often find themselves better situated to take on new ideas and try new skills. In the area of online music pedagogy, those instructors with growth mindsets are often better positioned to adapt and adopt new methods and approaches in their teaching – and with positive outcomes.

When we think about the rapid transition to online teaching as required by the 2020 pandemic, there were changes that impacted our physical environment, our teaching approach, and the amount of technology use in teaching. As a result, we can likely recall many instructors found themselves experiencing some level of burn-out, frustration, or at the least exhaustion. The amount of change required helped ensure students had the best possible learning experience during perhaps what may be defined as the most difficult event in their lifetime.

It is important to acknowledge the extreme challenge this event presented for music academics. They quickly adapted and learned new teaching approaches in a short amount of time. Many found themselves teaching online for the first time. No small feat. There were many difficulties along the way; however, there were also positive outcomes. The overwhelmingly positive outcome of the pandemic was the opportunity for many to expand their knowledge in pedagogy and begin to explore new ways to teach music in higher education. Some even found they not only enjoyed teaching music online, but that they found online activities and technologies that helped better support their students than their previous F2F teaching formats.

Many new online teaching practices have been shared due in part to our contemporary world as a connected culture through the internet. An inclusive pedagogical design is paramount so that people of many languages, cultures, and countries can experience social inclusivity through online music education. Yet, there is no quick fix or solution for learning how to teach online effectively. Furthermore, like any worthwhile teaching approach, it takes time to design an online music course that can effectively support and engage students in their learning. The process, while perhaps daunting to some, is not impossible. However, it does take planning and preparation. It is my hope that this framework provides a helpful starting place for those seeking to explore the opportunities of teaching music online. We may encounter various challenges and opportunities in our personal learning journey – yet step-by-step we can reach the goal set before us.

Envisioned through a social constructivist lens (Bandura, 1981; Vygotsky, 1978), the framework responds to instructional course design, communication technologies, and pedagogy as informed by appropriate research and practice.

Further, the framework addresses effective learning practices for both individual and social learning contexts within the definition of meaningful learning for artists as described by Csikszentmihalyi (1990).

The framework itself is a result of research from multiple studies in online music teaching and research literature across music education, online learning, and educational technology. A multiple-case study approach (Merriam, 1998; Yin, 2014) was used to systematically guide and frame the research. The multiple case studies involved a three-phase method of data collection and analyses. Students and faculty (i.e., online instructors, instructional designers, and administrators) from three Bachelor of Music programmes were invited to participate in the study. Case One had twenty total participants from a sampling frame of sixty (n = 20), Case Two had three total participants out of a possible twenty (n = 3), and Case Three had six total participants from a possible ninety-five (n = 6). Across the studies, students, instructors, and administrators were involved in completing online surveys, semi-structured interviews, and focus groups. Interviews and focus group questions focused on community knowledge and engagement, peer-to-peer learning, scalable teaching environments, and how transformative learning may impact and inform the various layers of post-secondary music education.

For those keen to get to the practical set-up and planning for teaching music online, you will likely skim the majority of the first section of this book. While the second section will provide helpful ideas to teaching music online, the enclosed case studies found in the first section will provide descriptive contexts that may help better elucidate your planning process.

Methodology

Case research is defined by Yin (2014) and Miles, Hubberman, and Saldaña (2014) to consist of a single, bounded unit, or phenomenon for social sciences study. This approach provides a means for implementing mixed methods (i.e., use of both qualitative and quantitative designs) data collection (Miles et al., 2014). Using a mixed method approach in a case study can bring together corroborating qualitative findings (e.g., interviews, journal entries) with quantitative data (e.g., survey data) (Miles et al., 2014). Furthermore, exploring the implications of a non-experimental design to collect data sources (e.g., surveys, interviews, reflective journaling and document analysis), case study affords a deep understanding of a unique unit of analysis (Merriam, 1998) with context-dependent knowledge building (Flyvbjerg, 2006; Yin, 2014). As Miles et al. (2014) further elucidate, multiple cases provide opportunities for 'confidence findings' (p. 33) that can be generalized within the context on which the case is theoretically based. Therefore, from this study, there can be possible generalizations made within the online music education context based upon social constructivism. Consequently, the strength of description gained by the case study approach will formulate an in-depth understanding of the research questions posed and provide rich examples and discussions of the online music education context.

Based upon multiple case research, the outcomes of the cases presented undergird the development of the framework (see Figure 2). To effectively demonstrate the overall research-informed process, specific aspects of each case are described after each component of the framework to provide the reader with multiple facets of examinations on the topic and support transparency of how the framework was developed from the three phases of each case.

Three phases of data collection took place for each of the three cases. During Phase One of data collection, participating students responded to the thirty-four-question Community of Inquiry survey (Arbaugh et al., 2008). These anonymous surveys sought to identify the effectiveness of online practices and tools of cognitive-, social-, and teaching-presences and provided a basic understanding of the effectiveness of teaching music online.

Specific examples of teaching and learning practices were further described by student and faculty participants through individual semi-structured interviews in Phase Two of data collection. Eight semi-structured questions were asked of students in confidential interviews. Similarly, a set of eight semi-structured interview questions were asked of faculty members.

The third phase of data collection provided opportunity for instructors and instructional designers to attend two one-hour focus group discussions at their campus location along with an option for faculty to attend via video conference. The focus group discussions with online faculty members explored the online teaching framework developed from the literature and data analysed from the previously completed Phases One and Two.

After the three-phase data analyses were completed, transferability (Polit & Beck, 2010) was sought through triangulation of data sources and triangulation of data collection methods (Creswell, 2012). Together, these data developed the practical framework concepts for teaching music in an online environment. These concepts were then brought to the individual faculty focus groups for final comments.

It is noted that online music education courses and BMus programmes are unique to each institution. Some programmes are part of a Fine Arts programme, whereas others are housed music programmes. Within various programmes and institutions, the number of online courses required for completion of the degree program may also differ. Since this study is on the phenomena of learning in the context of an online music course (i.e., not specific degree programme hierarchies), it is understood that the differences in institutional program requirements will not affect the outcome of data collection on components involved in online music education.

Significance of the Framework

Suggesting both practical outcomes of design efficacy for the educator and more meaningful learning outcomes for the non-localized students, a research-based framework for post-secondary music education can benefit the current and future music community. Such connections go beyond learning theories to identify essential components for effective delivery of online music education and promote both a more effective learning environment for the student and a practical understanding of implementation for educators.

Online music education research affords support to the interdisciplinary complexities of program sustainability and accessibility by providing a framework to guide the development of quality online music education. Signalling both practical outcomes of design efficacy for the educator and more meaningful learning outcomes for non-localized students, the resulting research-based framework for postsecondary music education has already been used by, and found beneficial by, the current online music education community. By making accommodations for the intricate balance of artistic learning and creativity in teaching (Csikszentmihalyi, 1990), it is posited that the resulting framework can respond to the immediate and future educational trends of higher education as outlined by Johnson et al. (2012). The significance of identifying essential components for delivery of quality online music education extends beyond the music discipline. One might say, if you can teach music online, you can teach anything online. While this may be an overstatement, it suggests the reachable attainment of inclusive and innovative learning in postsecondary contemporary learning environments for the betterment of overall student and faculty learning.

Online music faculty require some form of pedagogical and technological guidance (i.e., professional development) in online music pedagogy during and after their transition to teaching music online (Johnson, 2017). Johnson's study evidences the need for online music faculty members to know how to transition to the online environment and what pedagogical practices are warranted for music learning within a specific discipline context. These findings are grouped into three categories which comprise the framework to be explored: Design (i.e., planning, organization, and accessibility of course design to support students' learning and well-being); Assessment (i.e., integration that allowed students to reflect on their work and engage in their learning with other students, informal assessment and feedback mechanisms, peer feedback, and self-assessment); and Communication (i.e., as critical element for effective presence and community, timing of communication, choice of technology tools, and clarity of communication approaches).

Many of the online teaching practices represented in the framework suggest the constructivist practices as found in traditional F2F music courses. However, as indicated by various researchers, online learning also requires detailed attention to purposeful course design construction to provide an effective learning environment for interaction (Garrison, 2011; Gunawardena & McIsaac, 2004; Harasim, 2000; Keast, 2009).

The basic framework (Figure 2) is a guide that provides three main elements (i.e., Communication, Design, and Assessment) with their subsequent categories for faculty members to consider as they develop online music courses.

One can think of the framework as a continuous cycle of development – there is always opportunity to revise or update an online music class when we incorporate ideas from personal self-reflection and student feedback. At the onset, each aspect of the framework allows for the faculty members to choose various ideas that may be pertinent to their course design. The framework gives faculty members opportunities to scaffold their courses through a recursive teaching process relevant to the topics of communication, design, and assessment.

Overall, the cases that informed the development of the framework identified that constructivist and social-constructivist learning approaches can take place within the online music courses represented. These findings further evidence the three components of the Community of Inquiry framework (Garrison et al., 2001): teaching presence, cognitive presence, and social presence. Specifically, constructivist and social-constructivist learning tasks allow for students to further their abilities of self-regulation and meta-cognition (Garrison, 2011). Learning designs were also further facilitated by a TPACK approach (Koehler & Mishra, 2009). This strategy was helpful to position the learning content within a supportive level of technology that furthered student learning while consistent with a pedagogical design.

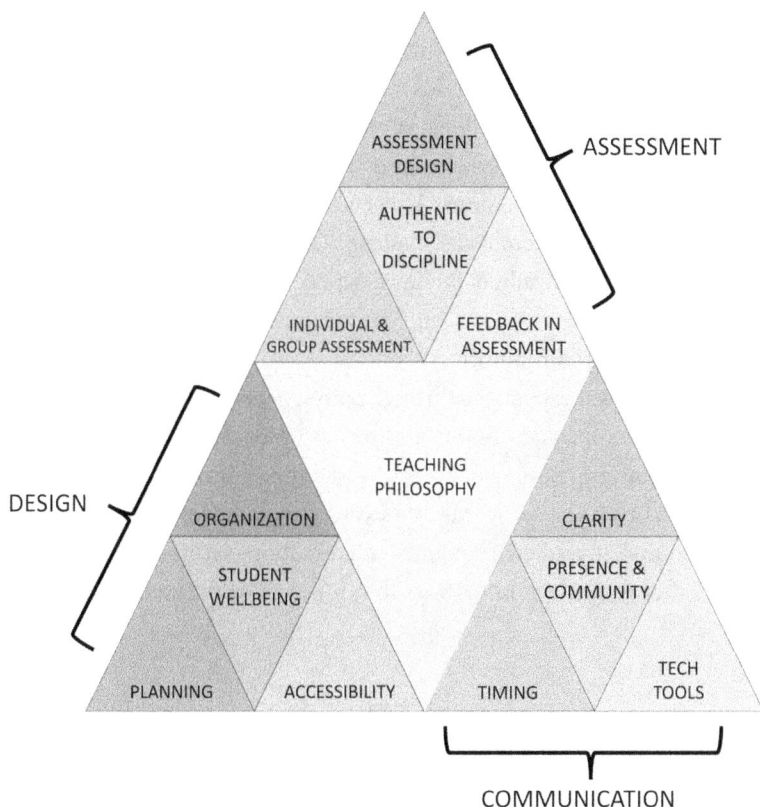

Figure 2 Detailed Framework for Teaching Music Online: Communication, Design, and Assessment Supported on the Foundations of One's Teaching Philosophy.

The following outlines the key results from the case studies in a brief overview. These summaries provide a helpful context as to the development of the need to address each of the main elements within each component of the framework.

Communication

There were many different forms and approaches to communication identified in the case study data. Key action items included clarity, timing, and a diverse, yet apparent, approach to presence and community. The key mechanism to ensure communication takes place is the identification of effective technology tools to use for each unique online teaching scenario.

Communication not only helped to address student motivation and isolation but was identified as 'absolutely' (Instructor, Case 3) integral for online music courses. A diverse use of synchronous and asynchronous dialogical exchanges were found across the cases. Students surveyed identified both a comfort with conversing within the online synchronous course activities and a comfort in participating in online discussions. However, there were notable challenges identified by the faculty members. Challenges noted by faculty included last-minute postings which resulted in limited peer interaction and a desire by students to complete learning tasks (e.g., get the grade and move on) rather than spend time in creating community.

Communication was exchanged through both synchronous and asynchronous technologies. However, synchronous sessions were identified as integral for an effective music learning outcome. Overall, communication was found not only to be a dialogical exchange of words, but expressions made through visuals and graphics. Community, and consequently collaboration, was found to be helpful for student learning, but was not always fully attained by the students.

Design

While each educator used unique and creative elements in their online music teaching, there was an overall process of Design that surfaced in the case studies. Four elements of design emerged from the case study results: Organization, Accessibility, Planning, and Student Well-Being.

Design brings together the entire learning plan to create a clarity for student learning. Planning and organization were provided through both visual course structure and content scaffolding. Further course design organization was provided through the articulation of course expectations by way of instructor-student interactions and course layout, and the consideration of how technology was introduced within the course design structure.

Finally, Re-design was a process that took place among faculty members both during and after course completion. It was integrated through conscious thought and actionable changes to course design. Re-design also involved simple actions, such as revising video links, through to larger re-vamping of learning tasks and content for better student engagement. Re-design was a process completed by both faculty using 'boxed' courses and personally created courses. Overall, the challenge of the time involved to design and develop an online music course was identified.

Assessment

The results of the case studies surfaced Assessment as a key component to online music teaching. Assessment was composed of four main elements: Authentic to the Discipline, Assessment Design, Feedback in Assessment, and Individual and Group Assessments.

The overall component of Assessment was found to include both formative and summative assessments as well as instructor self-assessments. There were a number of formative and summative assessments identified by the faculty members. Of particular importance to the assessment was the inclusion of content and assessment scaffolding, constructivist and the use of discussion forums for social-constructivist learning exchanges. Furthermore, group learning tasks were used and found helpful to encourage student membership in the course while creating a place for peer interaction that supported both social-constructivist learning and supportive learning networks.

Instructor self-assessments were completed informally by reviewing completed learning tasks by students to see how they aligned to the learning content presented. As a supportive resource, faculty members also used learning analytics available from their learning management system to better understand student challenges and opportunities with their learning tasks and overall course content design.

Challenging Our Assumptions

Drawing upon the literature for effective teaching in higher education, music education, online learning, and instructional design, we are faced with the opportunity to challenge common assumptions that may be present in our music conservatoires and departments, if not in our own thinking. There are three assumptions that I would offer you to consider as the framework is revealed throughout the book: (1) What if online music learning enabled more individual student learning?; (2) What if online music learning enabled more opportunities for students to interact with peers and professionals?; and (3) What if online music learning could be prepared to enable more efficient time on task? Throughout the narrative, these questions will be explored as the three-part framework of communication, design, and assessment is explained.

2

Communication

Introduction

We have likely all felt the impact of the 2020 global pandemic in our teaching. The adoption and required use of online teaching for many subjects, including music, were literally an overnight shift for many teachers. It is suggested that many music schools and conservatoires were caught off guard with instructors having a limited awareness of how to teach music online. Research in general academia (Rampanta et al., 2020), as well as music (Daubney & Fautley, 2020), highlights the limited pedagogical support instructors available prior to, and during, the pandemic to take up the dramatic paradigm shift to teach music online. This is a necessary pedagogical paradigm shift required to teach music online (Johnson, 2017). Therefore, it is understandable that many instructors felt frustrated with their limited knowledge or support for transitioning to an online teaching environment. A key component in teaching music online, communication, is important to both the development of online music classes and any mass-scale change in teaching approach. Communication is an important tool in change management (Senge, 2006) and very applicable for ensuring educators, as well as students, encounter success through transition and transformation.

Communication plays an integral role in our learning, and especially during times that require rapid response. Successful communication is clear, timely, evidences appropriate integrations of technology, and gives us a sense of connection to community. Pro-active and scaffolded communication plans provide those going through the change with goal posts for transitions, and strategies for successful achievement of those goals. It is from these points that we explore how to communicate well when teaching music online.

Communication

We use communication to inform and teach ourselves of the world around us. In a higher-level approach to how we learn, Root-Bernstein (2001) examines how transdisciplinary thinking informs our interpretation and learning of our current world. At this meta-level, the realities of patterns, syntheses, and observations can combine to communicate broad approaches to engaging in learning. For example, although a non-musician may not be able to perform a notated string of 16th notes on a page of music, the visual images of notes as ascending circles are themselves a pattern that a non-musician can interpret as an ascent of pitch.

Musicians communicate both through verbal means and through their musical creativity and musical performance. The opportunity to express both verbal communication and music communication is integral to musician learning. From this context, we need to ensure that students have opportunities to communicate in both these forms of language as necessary.

Although we may not consciously think about how we use meta-level communication systems and data, our mind is constantly helping us interpret symbols, sounds, graphics, body language, and the like. From this we can understand further how communication is at the core of teaching. When we teach, we typically use communication mechanisms that are associated with our discipline. In the discipline of music, we find ourselves using music, both music-as-notation and music-as-sound, as a communication tool. We also find ourselves using a 'cross-pollination' of our prior experiences and knowledge base to support our communication and approaches for communicating.

One of the main approaches to communication in the online environment is through video. As instructors, we create videos for multiple applications. This includes videos as supports student learning, performance videos, and project videos as assessments to evidence student knowledge. And, sometimes we incorporate video as a stand alone communications tool to communicate (e.g., student-to-student, student-to-teacher), rather than using alternate technology tools such as the phone or email.

Using video requires more time and technology involvement when compared to a F2F conversation or F2F teaching experience. We spend time locating a video tool and learning how to use it. We may need to plan talking points ahead of time, or even build a slide deck for visual cues. There is a lot of effort and time placed into video creation. However, we likely put in a similar level of effort into the crafting of a perfect teaching class – yet video creation requires time that happens as a 'front load' item.

While videos can support students in multiple review learning opportunities and be re-purposed for other classes, there are challenges that we encounter with video. Once completed, sometimes a video representation may not provide our goal of personal representation. A video may not capture the best representation of who we *feel* we are. These perceptions and feelings are valid. However, I would like to suggest that there are likely some underlying assumptions that may undermine our initial approach to video communications. Exploring these assumptions may slightly shift how we consider, and plan, for communication using video.

Assumption 1: Creating videos increases our teaching workload

As we look to the use of video in music performance learning on campus, there are some assumptions that need to be unpacked. First, there is an assumption that the creation of a video can take longer time to record and edit than its text-based counterpart. While it could take instructors longer in their initial video feedback creations, similar to any repetitive action, we develop a rhythm and planning routine that enables effective time management. One of the benefits of taking time to create videos is the opportunity for more targeted feedback to be given when compared to text feedback. Students can hear our voice inflections which positively influence how the feedback is perceived, and therefore taken up, by the student. When we explore the time and workload for creating video feedback, it has been evidenced that while the initial videos may take a few minutes to learn the technology tools used for video recording, the repetitive use of a single technology tool means that the learning curve incurred by the video application use decreases over time (Johnson & Blackburn, 2021).

Assumption 2: Using video in teaching requires tech savvy skills

A second assumption is that recording video feedback requires teachers to be equipped with technological savvy skill sets. This assumption is based on the notion that all technology requires a high level of technology knowledge. Those new to recording technology can explore simple recording tools that do not have, or require, detailed editing functions. For example, a video recording tool like www.screencast-o-matic.com, or the free Quicktime application on Apple™ devices, can provide an entry point for any level of user to record a video. For those wanting more elaborate and 'swish' videos, video editing software such as Camtasia or Final Cut Pro are available. However, simple video recording tools are effective for recording video feedback.

Assumption 3: Video use means flawless narrative

The third assumption to address is the notion that an instructor must provide a flawless speaking narrative in the video feedback itself. This assumption is linked to our natural comparison of our feedback video to a Hollywood movie. However, with over fifteen years of experience, I have found that students do not expect the instructor's video feedback to be seamless and without 'umms' or 'ahhs' in it. We have research that highlights how video feedback can provide students with key elements such as support, teacher care, motivation, clarity of meaning in feedback and provide means for students to be more reflective (Henderson & Phillips, 2015) and prompt change in future learning tasks and assessments. All of this can be effectively communicated with a couple of natural 'umms' – and even a bird chirp or two!

As we continue to reflect on our underlying assumptions in our overall teaching, let's also take time to explore how we can effectively communicate with our online music students.

Key Framework Considerations

The following section addresses the detailed aspects of the communication component of the Framework for Teaching Music Online (see Figure 3). There are four key considerations to communication: Clarity, Presence and Community, Timing, and Technology Tools. Together, these considerations integrate with the Design and Assessment components to help support an effective online music course for student learning.

Clarity

Simple, easy to understand. These are attributes of clarity of communication. They are effective because it affords simplicity and simple elegance. In a world culture that often texts in short 140 character statements, succinctness and precision are penultimate skills for the technology-minded. Clarity in itself also provides us with clear direction and order. When we consider clarity of communication for online music teaching, it also suggests the use of clarity in choice of technology and tools used to support clarity.

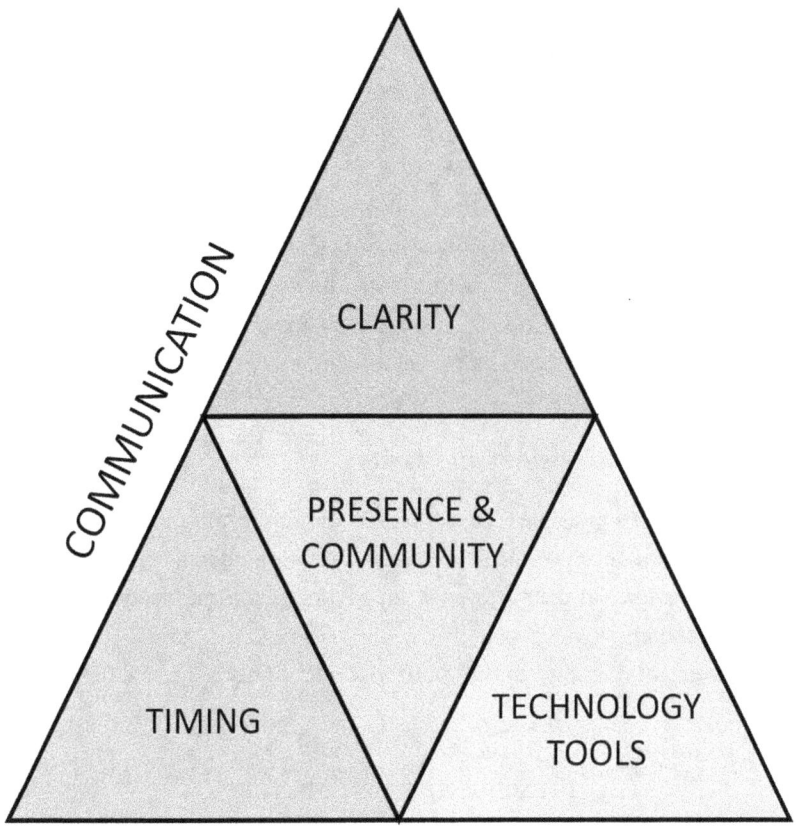

Figure 3 Key Considerations of Communication in the Framework for Teaching Music Online.

Clarity of communication can involve the use of multimedia. This may mean the use of a simple spoken word and transcript aligned with slow moving images and graphics that visually represent the spoken text. For example, students new to an online environment may not have experience with navigating an online LMS area. Use of a short one-minute orientation video can provide students with clarity of direction and understanding of ways they will be able to effectively communicate with the instructor and fellow students in the online class.

Clarity and communication are supported through a combination of visual and auditory considerations (Mayer, 2014, 2019). The identification of ideas and strategies for student reflection and future improvement was found to be perceived helpful for students when they viewed video (Borup et al., 2015). Furthermore, the use of video exchanges between student and teacher can also be supportive means for communication.

We support effective communication through the tools we use, as well as the assessments we choose. Students must be able to represent and communicate their knowledge of the topic and course content in their assessment itself. From this perspective, communication is an integral part for ensuring effective teaching in the online music course.

Finally, clarity of communication is also evidenced in how web pages are set up through their use of headers, fonts, colours, and page layouts. A streamlined and clean-looking web page provides students with further clarity that goes beyond mere text. It expounds on the expectations instructors have for overall communication and it becomes a model for students to replicate.

Key Questions to Consider on Clarity

- How have I used multiple forms of representation to communicate?
- To what extent does the LMS course area provide students with easy navigation and clear instructions to support clear communication of learning content?
- To what extent does my communication model clarity in my online teaching?

Presence and Community

One of the key approaches to attain effective communication is by creating and maintaining, presence. We can create presence in our online classes in multiple ways, including how we plan and implement video communications. Many use video conferencing software exclusively for the synchronous (i.e., real-time) teaching component when teaching online. This communication vehicle allows students to see and hear their teacher. And, if students' videos are switched on, they can all see each other. Seeing facial expressions, hairstyles, and choices of video background are all aspects that can support how our social self can make connections with others. There is a similar connection when we hear someone else talk – our ears connect accents and verbal descriptions that further support mental remembrances to the notion of place and presence. When we think of presence, it is this understanding that there is embodiment and an experience, or feeling, that someone is in the room. This 'in the room feeling' which is a virtual connection to place is made through eye contact, acoustic or sound environment. We are making affective connections – akin to when in person.

However, the reality is that the online environment can be challenging for some to feel presence. Oftentimes, this challenge is due to a perceived idea that the use of a web camera and monitor promotes only a limited social connection due to the lack of physical presence. However, in the online environment, the web camera is our eye into the virtual world. While we do not 'see' through the web camera, when an instructor looks and speaks directly into a camera, this can support of the visual experience of eye contact being made with the receiver/student, at the other end. That is, when we look into the web camers, the student on the receiving end experiences us looking directly at them on their monitor. While this may be initially awkward for the instructor to undertake, the practice enables students to perceive a form of teaching presence wherein the video connection supports better student engagement in the online activities and learning (Brandstrom et al., 2012).

If you want an activity to personally experience this notion of video presence, take a moment to record a short video where you talk directly into the web camera. Then record yourself talking to a distance beyond the camera lens. Watch both videos in replay. You will likely notice that you feel more engaged, or 'presence' from the video portion where you were looking directly into the camera. It's not a trick. Our brains affectively connect to someone more so when we perceive they are talking directly to us.

Video

To support the exchange of, and engagement in, online synchronous discussions, it is important for instructors to demonstrate the relevance and affective connection possible when video is enabled. Research evidences that students feel more connected to the instructor when the instructor has their video turned on during *synchronous* discussions and online activities (Johnson & Blackburn, 2021). When video is disabled, viewers perceive a decreased level of trust with the speaker. There is a form of disconnect when there is a voice without a visual image. Together, the use of video with audio provides the viewer with opportunity to hear vocal inflections and see facial expressions to inform their interpretation of teaching content. The instructor is observed by the students as modelling the expectation of online presence. This underscores the importance for instructors to ensure their internet is stable enough to transmit both audio and video in a live-streamed teaching session.

The sharing of one's image by video is a demonstration of trust to the recipient(s). This is particularly evident in student engagement through video.

While some students may find it awkward at first to have video on during synchronous discussions, the creation of a safe and trusting online teaching environment can often support students to turn on their web cameras during class. Smaller class sizes and the use of multiple breakout room activities can often support the nurturing of connection. Similar to the face-to-face environment, when students begin to connect with each other virtually, they are better positioned to trust one another.

Virtual Backgrounds

How we present ourselves online provides others with a visual and aural description of who we are and how they may perceive our connection to music. The use of a virtual background can also provide a perception of who we are to our students. Similarly, for some students, the use of a virtual background provides an opportunity to communicate freely while surrounded from a home environment in which they might not want to others to see. For example, some web cameras might have a wide lens that can capture more than an office/work area. Our video background makes up our online persona of who we are, and who students are, online. Welcoming students to represent themselves by their virtual backgrounds can support privacy and safety while encouraging communication. For some students, a virtual background can be a lifeline for opening up effective communication.

Key Questions to Consider on Presence

- To what extent do you look for ways to support presence and community during your online synchronous classes?
- How can you cultivate presence in an asynchronous class format?
- What is one new approach that you can consider so that presence and community can be furthered in your online music teaching?

Timing

We all have times in our life where we would like to stop the clock and have extra time. In the online teaching environment, we want our communication messages to seamlessly happen quickly and efficiently. For example, we may need to send out a reminder announcement to all students during the week, or we may need to quickly address a technology issue during a synchronous class. However, effective communication can take time to craft. We have likely all been there when the lack of clarity in an email communication was misunderstood and created further communication and possible deescalation.

Timely and effective communication can be supported by one practical principle: take time to re-read each email from top to bottom to ensure accuracy. If we don't take time to re-read your email, there will likely be a reciprocal email that will require a more time intrusive response. While not trying to make light of the busy administrative tasks instructors have placed upon them, there is a lot of truth to that last statement. If we don't take time to communicate well, it will cost us more time in the end.

Timing is also supported by transparent communication expectations. Setting expectations for email response time with students (e.g., twenty-four to forty-eight business house) can be outlined in syllabus and in the LMS instructor contact area. Outlining such expectations also signals a likely modelling of expectations for your students in return. We can provide healthy self-care boundaries such that it ensures we have some amount of flexible time to address urgent matters that may arise from time to time.

Feedback

Students are interested in their assignment feedback and grades. This can sometimes impact their level of communication to the degree that they are concerned. Setting and announcing your expectations for completing feedback and grades after an assessment has been handed in can also support a healthy and positive student community.

Key Questions to Consider on Timing in Communication

- What are the outlined time expectations for you to return an email to a student?
- Where is this expectation listed on your syllabus?
- What is the turnaround expectation for grades in your school or department? Is this specifically outlined in your syllabus or department website?

Technology Tools

The use of online learning in higher education provides students with opportunities for supportive learning approaches such as inclusive learning, curriculum differentiation, and necessary digital literacy skills for future employability. The adoption of online learning in higher education is now common across the globe as students embrace its flexible and accessible convenience. Specific to music, research further confirms online learning technologies support the effectiveness of learning music (Draper, 2008; Hammond, 2005), musicians' community needs (Salavuo, 2006), and the development of deeper music learning and cognitive skills (Dye, 2007).

The LMS itself houses well-developed communication tools. Examples of these tools include: LMS email, course announcements, institutional announcements, personal notifications, calendar, discussion forums, course module pages, in a variety of app plugins. These tools allow students to communicate with each other, with the teacher delete instructor, and with their learning content.

The technology tools themselves can support both asynchronous and synchronous communication, depending on the tool. For example, an instructor announcement is asynchronous and allows the student to choose how to receive and view the announcement itself. This supports student autonomy and leads to learner motivation. Video conference links support synchronous communication for students with instructors and classmates.

Communicating Music with Technology

To further how we communicate with technology tools, instructors should include technology tools that support discipline-specific nomenclature and lexicon. We find ourselves using typical tools found in other academic faculties across the university (e.g., LMS, video conferencing technology). The nature of music, and its performance and written form, also requires the search for additional discipline-specific technology tools to use when teaching online. This may mean that, as instructors, we adopt a new technology tool that clearly supports the content (e.g., music notation) we need to convey. It also may mean that we need to demonstrate how to use a software program, or add feedback on completed music assignments and activities. For example, when a student submits a composition activity, there may be a need to relay a correction on the composition to the student. The composition may be in an audio format, or a video format. To address the correction for effective communication (i.e., detailed, and authentic to the particular aspect of music), the instructor may need to use two technology tools at once – a recording application that 'plays' the audio or video, and simultaneously have another application opened so that the instructor can talk, annotate, or demonstrate the correction.

The use of multiple technology tools at once may seem complicated. However, if we envision the items as two separate activities (i.e., writing with notation software, and then recording the screen desktop), it is often less complex.

One of the most helpful approaches in online music learning mentioned by students through anecdotal evidence is the use of Zoom rooms for practising and providing peer feedback. The end result of these types of collaborative activities should focus on positive and supportive information that will help students improve in their musicianship.

Example 1: In small groups of two, students can perform for each other, or if one student is muted, they can perform duets. Once students have played together, they can give each other peer feedback. Students unfamiliar with this type of exercise may need exemplars or questions to guide them in giving effective critical peer feedback.

Example 2: In small groups of three to five, students can enter an online video conference space and take time to perform for each other. Alternatively, students can use this time as focused practice time wherein all students are on mute with videos on. For some students, this is a helpful accountability mechanism.

Key Questions to Consider on Technology Tools in Communication

- To what extent can you implement new music technology tools/plugins in your LMS?
- What is your institution's web page that outlines all acceptable use technology tools for communication across the university?
- What expectations have you outlined in your syllabus with regard to the use of technology tools in your class?

Next Steps

Communication is a multifaceted component that is intricately woven into the components of design and assessment. As you consider your next steps in developing your online music course, consider how communication is evidenced and expected through the considered approaches within design and assessment.

Questions for Personal Implementation

Key questions for the incorporation of communication have been outlined above. Consider the following foundational questions with regard to implementation of communication in your online music course:

- What is your 'go to' technology tool for relaying information to students? To what extent can you extend communication to ensure it supports at least two or three multimedia representations?
- When needing to address concern or tenuous points with a student, what are supportive communication tools to ensure and equitable and inclusive discussion?
- When you consider timeliness of communication, what expectations do you have for yourself?
- What expectations do you have for yourself and for your students?

3

Communication: Case Studies

According to case study data, the approach to effective and supportive communication in online music courses required instructors to integrate the use of specific technology tools in their teaching design. These included the use of discussion forums to initiate the building of student community at the beginning, middle, and end of the semester. However, students often interpreted the discussion area as an assessment activity rather than an opportunity for building community. Students also found the online environment to be an abstraction due to its lack of physical presence. Through the incorporation of careful communication of course design and technology expectations, student engagement and motivation for interaction and community could be increased.

Overall, developing community in an effective and sustainable manner was challenging for instructors new to teaching online. The use of various activities and technologies, such as discussion forums and Twitter, etc., were found to be helpful for some students, but not all. The interaction that is easily possible within a traditional classroom space required thinking differently about communication style, tools, and integration of community. As explicitly noted in Case 3, some students strongly suggested that they were taking an online class so that they could complete the class and not need to take part in developing community within the class. A multi-pronged approach that included embedding interactive discussion expectations and/or activities within the learning design was noted as supportive.

Students surveyed indicated that technology in online assessments and activities was found favourable. Quizzes and tests taken at home provided a more comfortable environment with less distractions. Students noted that there in-class tests were found more stressful than home online tests. While some students noted the convenience of online quizzes, online quizzes were also found to support student preparedness as well as immediate feedback through quiz grading outcomes. Overall, online students expressed a positive experience with the LMS, and chose to attend online lectures regularly.

Case 1

In this case, all online classes were taught both synchronously on-campus in a regular classroom with online students live-streaming via video conference (i.e., dual-mode teaching). One student described her classroom typically set up with students in their classroom desks facing the instructor at the front of the room, and an internet-connected web camera positioned on a tripod at the back of the class. The web camera was the classroom field of view for online students. Its capture provided online students with a full view of the classroom with audio, including the students and instructor in the room.

Students in the physical classroom space were able to speak to online students by unmuting their personal laptop device and speaking into their own computer microphone or providing commentary by typing text. All in-class audio and video communication took place through the live-streaming app within the university's learning management system (LMS).

Overall, the hybrid, or dual-mode delivery inherently created a sense of two distinct communities for students – one online and one on-campus. From this duality, there were apparent differences with regard to challenges of communication (i.e., how to connect with others online) as well as the development of a sense of community as a whole.

Finally, five out of the seven faculty members identified in Case 1 had an overall positive attitude as they transitioned from a traditional face-to-face format to online teaching. Previous technology course integration, personal interests in technology, previous classroom teaching experiences, and formal technology coursework were identified as examples of positive precursor experiences for teaching online.

Clarity

One of the key highlights noted by students was the need for clarity of expectations and direction in the online course area. Students reiterated the importance of having multiple due dates highlighted in different places within the online course area. The use of calendars and checklists was found to be supportive tools for clarity. Frustration was noted by students when assignment directions were too brief or lacked easy access to assessment criteria in rubrics.

An intuitive online design was found to be a supportive approach for bringing clarity to student learning. Clean and easy-to-navigate web pages and folders were preferred. The use of hyperlinking text to activities, discussions, and modules within the online course area was found useful for supporting student clarity.

Finally, the use of calendars and checklists reiterated course clarity for students. This provided students with explicit due dates that were directly linked to assignment directions. Weekly checklists that identified readings, activities, and/or tasks that needed to be completed were found to be helpful time management tools.

Timing

Because of the dual-mode class delivery, the timing of communication exchanges was experienced differently by on-campus and online students. This meant that face-to-face students were easily able to communicate with the instructor during class, while online students felt relegated to more communication through email. The timing and purposefulness of overall student-to-student conversation also appeared distinct within the sections.

Students from both the on-campus class and the online streamed area experienced a different timing of communication with their instructors and fellow classmates. Expressing a notable separation of communication between students in-class and online, one student highlighted how connections were easily made with students in-class before and after classes due to the opportunities of co-location. That is, walking into and out of the classroom provided students with opportunities of casual conversation or extended discussion about class activities and lessons. Online students found themselves trying to connect with other online students via email that occurred outside of class time. This suggests that students in the face-to-face environment had easier access to communication in a synchronous setting whereas the online students depended on the asynchronous nature of communication overall.

Students highlighted that they often chose the online programme due to the challenge of distance. Additionally, some students felt that the online programme also provided a novel factor for motivation. One student in particular viewed her motivation in the online learning classroom was perceived differently than her face-to-face classes. She stressed that there was a noticeable difference in how she approached her online classes and that overall student motivation for successful learning will increase when in a fully online class rather than a dual mode, or hybrid class scenario.

Presence and Community

Each faculty member expressed unique ways and emphasis on community development. One faculty member expressed his purposeful focus on community as it relates to learning when he expressed, 'Having everybody there, as much as possible, through different means of presence is the number one thing there.' This emphasis of synchronous community connections was found to be an optimal way to develop community. Emphasis on trying to have students talk real time during live-streaming was supported through audio and text chat. Having students connect with each other by video to see each other's faces was also seen as an important support for creating community.

Keys for the use and inclusion of various technology tools to develop community were described by Case 1 students. One student stated, 'I really think it's important for students ... Not just work through everything through text and through writing, but also through speaking and seeing each other, I think is also important.' Students described their learning together in an online course as going beyond a dialogic conversation and connecting with each other visually. They also described themselves as being 'pretty involved because they're always typing in the chat and asking questions.' Furthermore, the online students expressed favouring the addition of avatars or photos along with students' posts and chat boxes, 'because it's hard to know who-is-who in a chat box, because you only know the people's names.' Akin to the earlier remarks expressed by faculty wanting to see student faces when they are teaching, students had similar desires to connect visually with other students.

Need for Equitable Student Voice

Case 1 instructors taught from the front of a dual-mode classroom and often used lecture slides as teaching aids. Slides were displayed on a projector for both on-campus and online students to view. For lecture classes, they placed their teaching notes in the LMS prior to the start of class. Classes often had activities that required student participation and interaction (i.e., sight singing, rhythm clapping). Only one instructor spoke about how he purposely crafted his teaching time to ensure online students were fully participating when class were larger than two students. Another instructor expressed difficulty in the ability for online students to effectively participate and alternate video recordings of activities were used to compensate for lack of class participation.

A sense of community was not apparent across both teaching formats. That is, students online did not feel strongly connected to those students in the physical classroom. One student remarked that they were Facebook friends with on-location students, but that's all. With many students describing 'low level' connection between the dual-mode classes, students identified an excitement when they could meet F2F.

One student found her community to be located within both on-campus and online students; however, it was noted by two other students that they found it challenging to hear and read questions or comments from online students in a way that could help form student connections. This suggested that there can be a feeling of separation between the on-campus student and online student communities when students are not provided with equitable voice in a dual-mode teaching scenario.

Purposefulness of Community

In general, faculty and students agreed that community was about making meaningful and personal connections across the dual-mode teaching format. One instructor stated, 'Everybody's part of [the community] … it's just not one section.' He further described that he expected inclusivity of connection between the dual-mode students. 'I treat them like they're one – and I want them to learn about each other in the class.' Students felt that the inclusive environment was encouraged through willingness to participate.

Online students remarked on the purposeful use of 'reaching out' to fellow classmates. One student described that while she did aim to reach out to other students from her class, there was a challenge of trying to connect with classmates outside of class time. Feelings of exhaustion – with regard to trying to reach out to online student – led many students to stop trying to make social connections outside of class. A notable 'separation of class and life' further separated social connections and did not allow for online students to experience continued discussions after classes unless both online students were willing to purposefully make time to communicate online. One student explained,

> It's kind of interesting, because I took four semesters of music theory with an online student and at the end of the fourth semester like, he added me on Facebook. But we never really did any projects together or anything. So, it's kind of a connection, but not really.

Overall, students in Case 1 viewed the concentrated effort of faculty to build community within the online course context as helpful for the building of the social connections within classes. One student described course community as attainable and reasonable. 'I was able to meet three different young people, which was nice. I was able to keep in touch with them.' This type of friendship was a specific outcome described by another student when she stated, ' … Especially the younger girls, they're all like, best friends.' Students interviewed further affirmed the intentionality and beneficial outcomes of faculty fostering their online community. One student expressed, 'I found that [online communication] to be very helpful because it's almost as if you are together sitting in the same class … helped us feel right there.' This supports that some students find community in the online environment attainable when students are willing.

Challenges within Online Community

During the faculty focus group discussion, members indicated that online students are far more critical to the instructors than face-to-face students. One faculty discussion member stated, 'What I'm finding with online students is that they are by far, more critical of things that I do.' Another academic explained that F2F students were not as critical as online students, 'because they know you and don't have the guts to do it.' Overall, students were found to be more forceful about what they expected of the online teacher, which affected the perception of online pedagogy and how faculty members approached their teaching decisions.

Technology Tools

Faculty used many technology tools to support communication in teaching during the semester. Within a synchronous presentation, faculty described using the following LMS conferencing tools: text chat, whiteboard, slide presenter, video, polling, screen sharing, audio, and raised hand icons. All faculty members described using email to communicate with their students. In addition to email, other communication tools such as phone calls, Skype conferencing, and text chat were also described.

Students spoke about how they became engaged in their learning through the inclusion of technology. They confirmed the use of multiple technology and recordings made an impact on their learning. One student stated, 'It was helpful when they would provide PowerPoint that summarize what you learned in class and then I can go back and reread the PowerPoint and then, like, take the test.' Another student explained, 'That also is like a great thing, that I like, is having a recorded class, though. Because when you do miss, even though you might not get the same, like learning experience you would get while in class, it's still a great way to catch up and figure things out.'

Approaches to Communication

The online students in the dual-mode class setting described themselves as connecting with other online students during the class through texting, as well as in online Facebook groups. Online students perceived synchronous text chat in the discussion to both online and on-campus students and the instructor during a live-stream as a form of student contribution. These students agreed that it was helpful to have an open commenting area to chat among the online students during the live class. However, on-campus students perceived the text form of communication as a classroom disruption.

Students further highlighted the need for timely feedback from instructors. One student explained, '[Timely feedback is] really helpful because you do [the assignment] and then you're corrected on it right away and then you can try again.' This student further suggested that both the LMS and email were appropriate feedback tools.

Technology Tools for Communicating Learning

Not surprisingly, technology was a common topic arising from the data corpus collected. Technology was viewed as both an opportunity and challenge, depending on varying factors that included user's technology skill level as well as how technology was designed into the learning.

Both faculty and student participants groups confirmed using various types of technology in all courses. The LMS was described as the main technology tool used. It was used for housing content (e.g., .pdf, .mp4, .ppt, and .jpg) and providing links to the internet for additional material and websites. One student remarked, 'We had websites for practicing writing out of minor scales and stuff on the key signature.' Technology tools for synchronous and asynchronous communication such as video conferencing, telephone, email, and voicemail were heavily used. Highlighting the extent of technology used, one student affirmed, 'Well, for this college, there's a good amount.'

Challenges of Technology Tools

Faculty members created their own instructional videos on performance skills. As one faculty member indicated, 'that's more difficult to do online to do those videos. But I can at least see them [the student's presentation] and do that.' Another faculty member remarked at how difficult it is to adapt to teaching in front of a computer. Some instructors described that they are constantly moving around to express musical concepts when teaching. Finally, one faculty member remarked that music education is still waiting for some technology to be adequate to be used in applied (i.e., studio) music lessons. In general, 'treat technology as any other learning tool but respect the time it takes to learn it and respect the time it takes to deliver in the medium.' A backup plan was suggested by two of the faculty members to aid in teaching online – 'You never know with technology – sometimes they're great and then so many times they just don't work.'

Faculty also described a need to be adaptable when using synchronous communication due to possible latency issues, so that the learning task was focused on the student and not on technology concerns. For example, one faculty member described why she chose not to include play-along situations in her online performance teaching:

> … because then they get confused even more because they're playing and they're already two notes away and you say 'now turn' and they're like, 'Oh, here?' And then you're like 'Oh, no, no, no. I meant that like two notes ago.' And I realized that that just isn't going to work. And so I don't really like to stop it. Just let them play – unless they are really having trouble and then I say, 'Okay, let's start again. You were doing this wrong so make sure you turn after that finger, or whatever.

Faculty were not the only ones expressing challenges in adapting to new technology tools. Students found that they needed to have specific technology abilities to be successful online music students. One student expressed, 'It was challenging all in itself just because, it was so much different.' Another student suggested, 'It was almost too much like "do this online thing," "do this online thing," and it was hard to keep up with. Just because there were so many different components every day.' The challenges of incorporating technology into teaching and learning were found across instructors and students, respectively.

Case 2

Communication was an integral component in teaching music online of the Case 2 Instructor, David.[1] A focus on clear communication was considered in all aspects of the course (e.g., design, assessment, and learning activities) and there

---

[1] Pseudonyms have been used.

was an expectation for communication to be a teaching focus. For example, multiple communication approaches were explicitly outlined in the course syllabus as expectations.

Careful thought about choice of technology use to instruction was provided by the instructor to help assist students on the use of technology for increased time management and effective course interaction. While the type of technology used was not mandated, a specific file format was required for students' activities submissions. Students found support from both the instructor and a librarian. Together, they were found to better inform students on ways to research and use university databases. They gave focused attention to ensure clear communication on technology use and overall class expectations were known.

The instructor used asynchronous and synchronous methods of communication. In both forms of communication, the technology tools used to communicate were found to be common and accessible for students. The form of the technology used appeared 'normal' to the students and was not considered exceptional or difficult to use. This meant that the communication tools were easily located in the current LMS and supported both one-way and bidirectional communication as needed. Examples of asynchronous tools used included: discussion forums, email, SMS text, and LMS announcements. The inclusion of lecture notes as text, and YouTube links for further explanations, was also viewed as valuable communication tools by the students.

The synchronous communication tools used by the instructor supported audio, video, and text. Focusing on the synchronous aspects, the tools allowed for bidirectional communication between instructor-to-student, and student-to-student. Students were encouraged to use synchronous tools inside the online class as well as outside of class time. Students communicated often with the instructor through a variety of synchronous tools: phone calls via Skype, FaceTime, and chat room, and live in-class online discussions.

Presence and Community

Instructor David took time to purposefully build community into his learning tasks by implementing group projects. He overtly stated, 'Community building is important.' Interaction was viewed to be the key to learning and as such, community was built into the activities and encouraged throughout the course. The focus of interaction as a key part of the learning experience was notable. Not only were students encouraged to connect with the instructor, but students were also encouraged to connect with each other. This was evidenced in the instructor's focused use of group projects at the beginning of the semester. The use of group projects allowed for new students to become part of the student membership quickly and established the expectation of community. Projects were designed to support the development of community and communication between students. This allowed for students to share their knowledge with each other and learn in a community environment (i.e., social constructivism).

The development of community among the students was identified as a form of 'good teaching'. It was acknowledged that the challenge of community development rests on the initial teaching design and teacher focus. Emphasis on community and consequential communication expectations for community development was a focus point in the first weeks of the semester. This tenet gave students a shared understanding and explicit awareness of not only how to use technology for effective communication but that it was an expectation within the class.

Technology Tools

There were a number of technology tools identified as being integral for effective communication within the online music class. The diversity of tools used (i.e., Skype, phone, email, SMS text, video conference, LMS) ensured that students had opportunities to engage in communication with a tool that they found comfortable to use. However, there was no specific mandate for students to use a specific technology tool.

A unique approach to ensuring students felt community was through the use of technology-enhanced discussion activities in the first few weeks of class. Students were given opportunity to help each other get used to and share technology tools through a small group learning activity. The development of a 'community safety net' was found to be enhanced when students were able to communicate with each other through multiple technology tools for communication.

Case 3

Case 3 had five instructors in total. Each instructor had different nuances and perceived the online classroom often as a comparison to F2F classes. With extensive teaching experiences in a variety of teaching scenarios, instructors found themselves open to the use of technology, keeping current with possible places for innovation in music classes, and an overall excitement for teaching music.

Clarity

The emphasis of clarity in communication was found across each of the five instructor interviews. Instructors aimed to provide students with explicit emails and LMS announcement communications that reiterated the weekly activities and upcoming assignments. The use of video communications and the format of short five-minute content videos for lectures were given as examples that provided students with additional clarity and ways to further support understanding of the course content.

Communication clarity was identified as challenging when it came to trying to rearticulate (i.e., restate) directions for assignments in the LMS area. In addition to text, the adoption of visuals, graphics, and video was used to support the clarity of assignment and announcement communications. One instructor in particular took to the use of weekly video announcements and felt that the adoption of the video announcement approach was perceived favourably and helped support student learning.

Timing

The use of weekly discussion activities prompted questions about timing in communication. For example, due to the nature of students posting asynchronously across the week, one instructor noted that 'some students would post right away, another student wouldn't show up until towards the end of the week'. The instructor further described her students as not allocating enough time to the coursework in general. Together, these experiences suggest that students may need further support (e.g., calendars or weekly checklists) as explicit communication activities throughout the week.

Presence and Community

Although there is inconclusive evidence as to why students post to the discussion area at different times of the week, one instructor highlighted that her students overtly stated, 'We don't want to be a part of a community. If we did, we'd take a physical class. We just want to take an online class that's it.' This surprising statement highlights the diverse reasons students take an online class and the necessary scaffolding structures of considered course design.

Technology Tools

Students at this university were open to attending optional live, synchronous communication with their peers. These synchronous sessions were held at the same time each week and in an informal 'café-style' manner. One instructor remarked, 'The students who participated, many of them said that they enjoyed it. They enjoyed having a live discussion. But just time-wise it was too challenging.'

The challenges of finding a technology that was liked by 100 per cent of the students in the course were noted by another faculty member as she tried to communicate with her students that already used Twitter. The instructor further expressed, 'I started a Twitter account … and told them to follow it.' However, she found out that students were not necessarily looking for more ways to communicate with their instructor. 'Some of them respond and take advantage of that, and some of them do not,' she explained. A specific approach was not found to resolve this challenge. Therefore, the instructor highlighted how she started using common social media networks to further engage her students with their course content learning. Notably, this instructor found that, overall, student participation was highly attached to students' grade and achievement levels. This suggests that a clear expectation of technology tool use for students needs to be integrated into the curriculum teaching itself for effective practice.

Questions to Consider

From the case studies it is apparent that there are multiple approaches to effective communication in the online environment. The cases highlight the use of a wide range of tools to ensure students have opportunity and skills to engage in communication. The examples above suggest that sustaining community in the online classroom is a continued activity across the semester.

From this perspective:

- What are two or three activities that you could incorporate in the first three weeks of your online class to support the development of community?
- Thinking across the semester, how might you be able to reasonably continue a weekly activity to engage students in community?

4

Design

Introduction

Although there are many different faces of online learning, the basic concept of online learning is that students receive instruction via an online learning environment and not a traditional, face-to-face classroom format. Visualized as a continuum with traditional face-to-face learning at one end and online learning at the other end, it can be understood that many permutations of online learning can, and do, exist (see Chapter 1).

The online learning environment gives students opportunity to engage in their learning through various different online technologies (i.e., asynchronous and synchronous tools). Appealing to students with the advantage of anytime learning, asynchronous learning resources and activities within an online learning environment may include, but certainly are not limited to: posting in discussion forums, viewing videos, listening to podcasts, submitting time-stamped assignments, etc. Online learning environments can also provide synchronous learning opportunities for students: real-time video conferencing, synchronous document creation, and live audio and/or text messaging. While there may seem to be an endless number of applications available to use in an online learning environment, the effective learning outcomes from the various tools become apparent when viewed through instructional design. Continually linking back to the online course's main learning objectives, the use of an instructional design framework will aid in determining which asynchronous and synchronous tools align to pre-determined course learning outcomes.

Based on traditional constructs of teaching (i.e., learning theory, instructional models, etc.), online learning uses the field of cognition and learning, to establish models for designing learning situations (e.g., from the larger programming of courses, down to smaller components of classes and activities).

For example, previous research demonstrates that different modes of knowing support the scaffolding of musical knowledge, learning and skills (see Elliot, 1995). Elliot identified four modes wherein musicians develop musicianship skills: formal, informal, impressionistic, and supervisory modes. Understanding that musical knowledge can be formed through different means, it is therefore reasonable to consider that before students listen to a work, a pre-performance dialogue needed to take place to foster intelligent listening. That is, cognitive listening to music is a necessity for developing musicianship. It is this notion of step-wise progression that becomes integral in music course design, and even more so in online music course design.

Constructivist Learning Design

Many educational scholars have sought to parse how to obtain an ideal learning presentation through instructional design models and theories. Set within an extensive research landscape, instructional design is described as a two-pronged theory that outlines situations and methods through identified desired outcomes and instructional conditions (Reigeluth, 1999), that addresses instructional events (Gagne & Driscoll, 1988), and the cognitive, affective, and psychological perspectives of learning (Maslow, 1943).

Jonassen (1992) further suggests that a person's self-experience is an integral component of learning as he writes,

> Constructivism is concerned with how we construct knowledge from our experiences, mental structures and beliefs that are used to interpret objects and events. ... Constructivism holds that the mind is instrumental and essential in interpreting events, objects and perspectives on the real world, and that those interpretations comprise a knowledge-base that is personal and individualistic.
>
> (p. 139)

Connected to the outcome of meaningful learning, the foundations of a constructivist instructional design support a framework best suited for the dynamic environment for online learning.

'As education researchers seek to increase the body of knowledge about effective teaching and learning, it is important not to neglect a critical variable in the instructional equation: course format' (Seamon, 2004). Instructors 'play a crucial role in students' knowledge construction by scaffolding the learning process for them' (Tallent-Runnels et al., 2006, p. 101). Although Tallent-Runnels et al. suggest there is a need for further control groups in their literature study to strengthen design and method, 'the majority of researchers agree that online instruction is at least as effective as traditional ways of teaching' (p. 105).

Self-Regulated Learning through Feedback

The attainment and use of self-regulation skills are the 'critical factor' (You & Yang, 2014, p. 125) for students learning online (Allen & Seaman, 2013). The relationship of self-regulation skills to online music assessment is further exemplified further by Ritchie and Sharpe (2021). In their study on conservatoire music performance students (n = 84) that transitioned classes to the online environment in the first two weeks of the 2020 Covid-19 pandemic in the UK, less than 23 per cent of students (i.e., nineteen students) chose to defer and forgo online performance assessments. Using previously established questionnaires that addressed self-efficacy, resiliency, and state of well-being state in multiple survey intakes, students exhibiting high self-regulation demonstrated remarkable resiliency which was linked to high levels of self-efficacy along with implementing multiple strategies to complete an online performance assessment (Richie & Sharpe, 2021). That is, 'The multiplicity of strategies and the use of self-directed learning to engage with resources, people, and to develop new skills aligns with expected behavior of people with higher self-efficacy beliefs' (p. 6). Overall, Richie and Sharpe's research suggests students scoring higher levels of self-efficacy and self-regulation skills for performance were found better situated to take up an alternate form of assessment. From this study, and others (Habe et al., 2021; Yildirim & Solmaz, 2020; You & Yang, 2014), there is a need for music instruction that seeks to purposely support and develop music students' mindsets for resiliency, well-being, as well as practical methods for self-regulation.

In their research on music performance and sport students, Habe et al. (2021) found 'Having clearly set goals, good feedback about one's performance, being pulled into the activity and thus experiencing a loss of self-consciousness, and experiencing transformation of time increase satisfaction with life but having the need to control events will decrease satisfaction with life' (p. 7). Therefore, openness for change (see Dweck's (2019) writing on growth mindset versus fixed mindset), low-load thinking time, and self-regulated learning are key approaches to share and encourage the development of our students. The need to ensure our teaching practice supports, models, and shares strategies for self-regulated learning is key.

Having explored the student engagement and motivation aspects in online learning, it appears that the additions of feedback, feed-forward and feed-up, plus online assessments that connect to student relatedness/motivation, could provide high learning/motivation outcomes for music students. McPherson (2022) and his recapitulation of the importance of self-regulated learning outlines how music educators need to help students move from that point on the continuum of extrinsic motivation to the right side of intrinsic motivation. We, as teachers, can do this by supporting students in teaching practices that encourage the development and use of autonomy, competence, and relatedness (McPherson, 2022).

Contextualized specifically to online learning (see Figure 4) we can observe that when students receive communication that develops corresponding levels of community, in combination with increased organizational design of the online learning environment and clarity and organization, stronger student engagement is achieved. Alternately, disengagement in student learning occurs when communication is unclear or the design in the online environment is limited. For example, when a student comes into an online learning management system

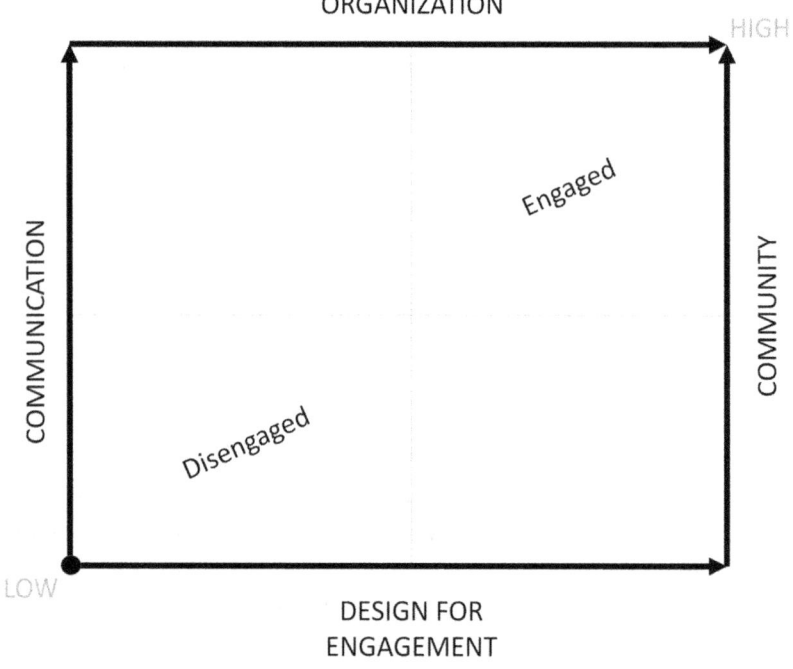

Figure 4 The Increase of Student Engagement through Considered Online Course Design.

that is intuitively designed, that is, students know where to locate the weekly modules assessment activities and overall directions for the class, students will have higher engagement.

Instructional Design Models

As we navigate the development of online music courses, instructional design models are helpful in the exploration of design (Branch & Kopcha, 2014). Helpful models for designing effective leaching experiences include: 'learning by design' (McTighe & Wiggins, 2012), the ADDIE model (Molenda, 2015), and the Community of Inquiry framework (Garrison, 2011). The following section explores these models that are found to be helpful in the construction of an online music course.

Learning by Design is the model highlighted by McTighe and Wiggins (2012). This model is useful as it focuses on the identification of the desired final results of learning. Through this approach, instructors look to the final results to determine the appropriate assessments that lead up to the attainment of the final learning outcome. Planned learning experiences, activities, and considered instruction are the focus points used to scaffold the learning from start to finish.

The ADDIE model (Molenda, 2015) is an approach that many may use without the realization they're using it due to its simplistic, yet systematic, nature. The ADDIE acronym stands for its five-step process of instructional design: analysis, design, develop, implement, and evaluation. When using this model to develop online courses, the first step of analysis ensures that the instructor is creating appropriate content for the topic. Analysis of the content knowledge as well as the audience is taken into account. The design step of this model is the crafting of an approach to conceive accumulative learning across the course. The implementation face consists of deploying the course to its intended audience. The final phase of evaluation requires that the instructor take time to identify opportunities and challenges that occurred during the course due to design structures. Comments and enquiries from students are important considerations to reflect upon during the evaluation stage. The final step of the process, evaluation, includes evaluations through student- and instructor-reflection and the redesign of the course itself.

The Community of Inquiry framework resulted from the research of Garrison et al. (2001). It was originally designed to support text-based discourse in teaching and learning online. Yet, this framework has been further used to explore the overall student-to-teacher to content interactions in an online course. Specifically, three components were found to be central for an effective online learning environment: teaching presence, social presence, and cognitive presence.

These three Community of Inquiry presences are represented by overlapping circles to highlight how each of these aspects requires, and is influenced by, each other. While the framework itself is multifaceted, the overlapping nexus of the presences forms teaching experiences that provide opportunities for explicit teaching presence, social presence, and cognitive presence to take place. Teaching presence does not only refer to a teacher being part of the class. It is also about the design of the teaching experience and how the student engages in the learning. The social presence is for students to have a socially constructed learning experience. And finally, cognitive presence is the opportunity for students to engage and interact with the content being taught in a sustained manner. The detailed Community of Inquiry thirty-four-question survey (Arbaugh et al., 2008) was created as an instrument to inform instructors of the extent to which each teaching presence was being addressed in an online class. An instructor can implement this survey for better understanding of students' overall perceptions on course design and engagement in terms of the three Community of Inquiry presences.

Strategies for creating and supporting the Community of Inquiry's teaching presence are furthered when adhered through a process of preparation, design implementation, and assessment of the facilitation (Johnson & Altowairiki, 2017). As we use considered practices that support these strategies, the connection and realization of cognitive understanding and meaning can support strong learning outcomes.

Together these models provide opportunity to develop learning experiences that are considered, purposeful, and carefully constructed for the learner.

Addressing Anxiety in Music Students

Studies concerning music students suggest the implementation of emotional and psychological support services (Perkins et al., 2017), in addition to preventative training of musculoskeletal injuries in musicians (Árnason et al., 2014), and healthy practices routines (Perkins et al., 2017) are necessary for conservatoire students. Faced with fixed performance deadlines and practice times arranged within a full schedule of music classes, music students experience stress and performance anxiety at a different pace and level than most university-level students.

Through semi-structured interviews with UK conservatoire students (n = 20), Perkins et al. (2017) suggested students perceive barriers within the conservatoire to include: lifestyle challenges, practice and learning challenges, low levels of health awareness, psychological distress, challenges with performance feedback, workload, among others. The results further indicate a '"need for continued work to embed health and well-being support as an integral component …" [and] "provide spaces for *learning* performance …. allowing students to connect with the aspects of performance that sustain well-being while minimizing the negative implication"' (p. 13).

In a study comparing music students to its other University of Freiburg faculties, Spahn et al. (2004) reported, 'Music students rated 8.4% in the HADS depression scale, and 33.5% on the anxiety scale, which was significantly more than the other students and placed them in the borderline or elevated range' (p. 26). Indeed, music conservatoires are at key junctures wherein addressing these health and well-being is not optional but necessary for the health of musicians, and for the integral sustainability of the conservatoire. Findings suggest there is 'a need for more radical scrutiny of the cultures of conservatoires and an assessment of how these can be modified to best optimize students' health and well-being' (Perkins et al., 2017, p. 1).

These students also have requirements to attend in-class lectures and music lessons, participate in multiple weekly rehearsals, and perform semester technical exams. Music students often spend time commuting to school, work to support their schooling, and/or have carer responsibilities. Together with the need to develop an entrepreneurial mindset for the known circuitous route of the entrepreneurial musician (Johnson et al., 2019), music students are often time poor which adds to their overall challenges to health and well-being. However, research has identified online learning as an equal alternative to face-to-face learning. For example, online music learning research has evidenced positive music student learning outcomes in both online music lessons for younger students (Dye, 2007) and online music tertiary subjects (Damon & Rockinson-Szapkiw, 2018).

Furthermore, in the Framework for Promoting Student Mental Well-being in Universities, Baik et al. (2017) reported five components that contribute to student health and well-being in tertiary education. The five areas are 'foster engaging curricula and learning experiences; cultivate supportive social, physical, and digital environments; strengthen community awareness and actions; develop students' mental health knowledge and self-regulatory skills; ensure access to effective services' (p. vi). Given the importance of these criteria for tertiary students, it is understood that online learning and teaching should also address and support online students' health and well-being.

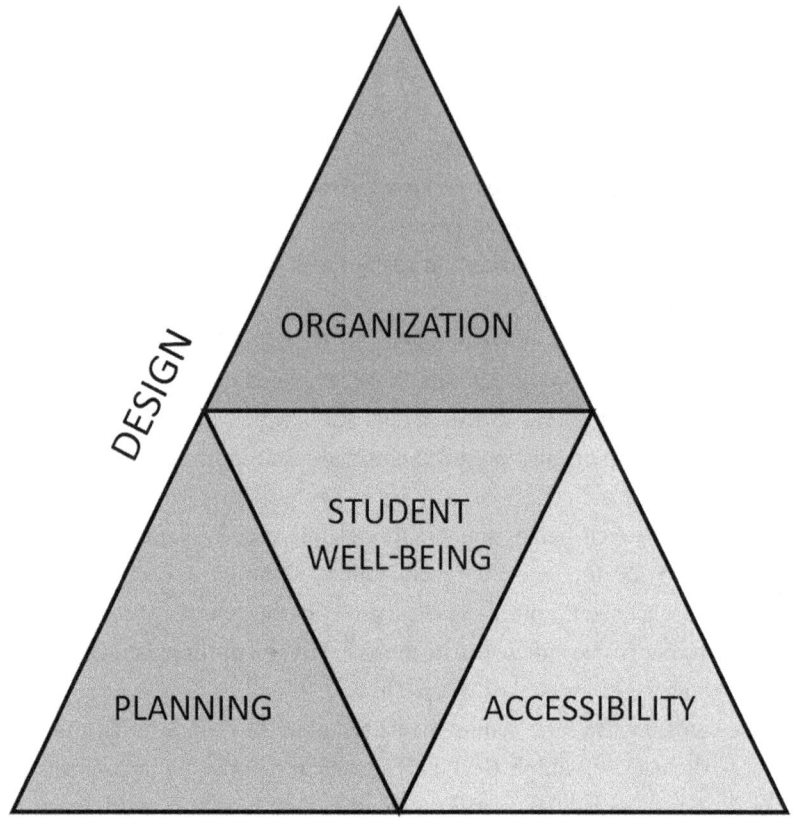

Figure 5 Key Considerations of Design in the Framework for Teaching Music Online.

Key Framework Considerations

The design component of the framework for teaching music online consists of four distinct interrelated considerations for creating effective online music courses: organization, planning, accessibility, and students' well-being (see Figure 5). Each of these considerations will be explored in the following section with an inclusion of recommendations for practice.

Organization

Organization is a supportive approach for any effective teaching event. Not only does organization promote clarity of direction, but it also provides the instructor and student with optimal navigate learning experiences supported by a design that is intuitive and predictable manner.

Organization in online music courses is often thought as relegated too specific development of modules and lessons. Yet organization of teaching starts with the larger learning objectives of the course. This considered design is then threaded through all aspects of the course itself.

Unfortunately, individual music instruction is often associated with less-than detailed lesson organization. In her book on teaching music performance, Sylvia Coats (2006) challenges this view and supports the need for all instructors to take up lesson planning. While focused on face-to-face teaching, the pedagogical paradigm shift required for the online environment demands careful organization and structures in place prior to students entering the online lesson area.

Organization can also address time management for instructor and student workload. Taking advantage of the efficiencies that come with the use of technology, the online music course can include weekly audio and video recordings to support the structure of the work week. Further use of pre-recorded and time released videos and announcements further the evidence of careful organizational design. Finally, using checklists to help students scaffold and chunk their activities is an additional effective organizational tool.

Ensuring students are aware of the time commitments required for successful completion of the online course is necessary. Highlighting expectations of time commitments also supports students in understanding necessary time management allocation.

Providing students with opportunities to highlight how they can find regularly scheduled offline time can also support student motivation through organization. One of the often-cited proponent studies supporting regularly scheduled offline time is Martinak (2012). In this study, results indicate support for taking one day out of seven as an offline day and limited working day. This offline day provides the body and mind with time to rejuvenate and be refreshed to once again start the workweek.

Organized Structure

When designing an online course for music, one of the most helpful aspects for student success is giving focus to how the course is organized and the structures used to evidence the levels of organization. The case studies further emphasized this need for detailed organization. Careful planning and development of the online area can support student learning success, as well as aid in overall workload management for the instructor. For example, setting up a landing page that highlights how students can easily navigate the online course, locate key links to resource areas, as well as specific ways to communicate with the instructor and collaborate with peers can be helpful LMS structure supports.

Organized and structured online class supports an intuitive and predictable design. This means that students will know how often they need to access the online area and if there are specific times wherein, they should log in. The use of the same password-protected video conference link further supports a predictable course design. Finally, the creation are they 'video course map' can visually guide our students through the entire online course area when they first arrive. A visual 'course map' essentially represents your course syllabus – it visualizes the content through a recording capturing a screencast tour of our online LMS class area.

To help aid your own organization and structure, it is helpful to consider strategies to ensure the storing of class content on the computer is organized in a manner that is intuitive and predictable. Easy location of files can take place when the folder naming system resembles the online course area. Consistent and reasonable naming conventions further aid easy file access (for example, see Figure 13).

Synchronous Performance Lessons

Similar to the live, on-campus studio lesson, a predictable and organized online studio lesson supports effective student learning. A predictable online lesson may start with a short welcome to the student, highlight student care (e.g., 'How are you doing'), and seek out any student challenges from the past week (e.g., 'Were there any difficulties in your practice time this week?'). To develop self-regulation skills, it is important to highlight the goals of the current lesson and request the student to take notes during the lesson.

Starting with a short warm-up, the student positioned and prepared to play specific repertoire in the lesson. Depending on the instructor's approach to teaching, the remainder of the lesson is often varied and likely includes student performance, discussions about historical performance practice, performance techniques, performance strategies, etc. Approximately three to five minutes before the end of the lesson, the instructor should begin to review new ideas talked about during the lesson. Allotting time for lesson closure provides the instructor with opportunity to review the highlight of the lesson time, and ensure the student is aware of the expectations and achievements for the next lesson.

Key Questions to Consider on Organization in Design

Key questions to explore with regard to organization are outlined below as you reflect on these questions, and consider how they will impact your choices in structural design of your online music class.

- How is the class organized? (e.g., Semester or Year)
- What are the learning outcomes that need to be achieved? How will you know they are achieved?
- What online platform or protected website are you using for organizing student materials?
- How often should students access the area?
- What will students need to retrieve from the online area?
- What are the main components for the online area? (Content Folders – Organized by theme, week, or student?)
- What folders should students see first or prominent in the online?

Planning

The planning of an online music class does not happen overnight. It requires considered thought, research of content, in mapping of curriculum objectives and goals. Planning is materialized in the overarching threads of discipline content, integrated projects and assessments, as well as overall cumulative scaffolding of content.

Scaffolding of Lessons

Routinely recognized as effective teaching strategies in the traditional school model, scaffolding and reflection are also successful tools used in the online classroom. Recall that scaffolding is the strategic learning process of incremental knowledge building. A systematic incorporation of inquiry-based activities can begin with a simple subject concept and add on to the activities through a stepwise progression until a larger concept is attained. Each activity is carefully designed to target ideas that will be needed for the next activity. From these stepwise ideas, the student is able to gain a deeper understanding of the material in bite-size, success-oriented increments.

Learner scaffolding is focused on starting with the basic knowledge components and constructing upon that knowledge across the semester. Scaffolds support both content learning and assessments towards the main learning outcomes.

Group and Individual Activity Planning

One of the things to consider in creating online activities is the use of individual versus group activities. In face-to-face music teaching, there has been much discussion over the adoption of group activities in studio performance teaching and learning (Bjøntegaard, 2015; Gaunt, 2007, 2010; Mitchell, 2020b). The challenges of, and the opportunities from, music students participating in group studio lessons are notable. However, as noted by Gaunt (2010), while the use of one-to-one studio lessons in F2F can decrease the feeling of competition across music students, there is concern students view those outside their lessons as merely personal contacts rather than additional learning supports. This suggests that students in one-to-one lessons may not consider their community of fellow musicians as a learning community, or Community of Practice. However, group music learning has shown to position students for shared learning experience, community, increased motivation in learning, and support leadership building (Bjøntegaard, 2015; Hallam, 1998; Mitchell, 2020b).

When thinking about teaching studio lessons online, we may assume that all online studio lessons are created as one-to-one studio performance lessons. However, what if online studio lessons included a rotation of online group lessons, across the semester of individual online lessons? Research outlines there are benefits of group F2F studio lessons and individual lessons (see Mitchell, 2020b). Building on this idea, it is suggested that the achieved outcomes of face-to-face group lesson could be attained in the online group lesson – when classes are appropriately set up for online teaching. Given the importance of detailed planning required for online music teaching, one could consider a rotation of online group music lessons to reduce the challenges known with regard to face-to-face studio lessons. That is, face-to-face individual lessons are often described by students as having 'periods of directionless activity observed in lessons' (Gaunt, 2007, p. 216), limited individual lesson planning by teachers (Coats, 2006), and students are described as having an overall teacher dependency (Gaunt, 2010). With a carefully designed online group lesson, students can gain similar learning outcomes akin to F2F group music lessons.

However, as noted in the research, individual and group lessons achieve different learning outcomes. Therefore, it is necessary to consider both the content chosen and design of activities for the online group lesson. In describing group lessons, Mitchell (2020b) suggests 'chord and scale knowledge, chord voicings and fingerings, all activities not dependent on individual feedback and attention' (p. 122), and overall content that does not rely on performance activities are appropriate content foci. As regularly scheduled classes incorporated across the online studio teaching timetable, such content could be easily explored, discussed, and designed for an interactive online learning experience.

Key Questions to Consider on Planning in Design

Key questions to address planning design include the areas of learning scaffolds and thoughtful exploration to determine appropriate inclusion of individual and group activities:

- How can the content be broken down into 'chunks' to build learner success and confidence?
- Where does teacher connection need to happen for learning support? Synchronous or asynchronous?
- How does the content relate back to the real-world discipline? How is this highlighted?
- What are the complex ideas that need additional forms of explanation?
- To what extent should the learning include individual and group activities?
- How can previous F2F group activities be transformed for effective online and interactive group activities?
- What activities work best as individual online activities, and what work best as group online activities?
- How are the online activities planned to support the final learning outcomes of the course?

Accessibility

Universal Design for Learning (UDL) (Meyer et al., 2014) is a research-informed practice that provides learners with experiences that allows the use of various multimedia. In a rather simplistic description, UDL is the use of multiple means of media so that students can show what they know and for teaching to affectively engage students through the use of video, graphic, audio, and text representations. Originating as an architectural approach to ensure everyone could access a building, architects created multiple ways for people to access a building. For example, the use of stairs, wheelchair ramps, and elevators provides a way for people to move from one area to another. In the same way, UDL uses multiple means of media to demonstrate and represent content in approachable ways for different learners. Through this simplistic description of its complex design of strategic networks, recognition networks, and effective networks, UDL offers learners multiple ways to access online learning.

Key Questions to Consider on Accessibility in Design

When exploring accessibility of online learning content, consider the following questions:

- To what extent does the learning activity provide students with opportunity to engage using text, audio, video, or graphics?
- To what extent can students use video or graphics as representation in their assessment responses?
- Have I provided a transcript for my videos?
- Where are the multiple links for students to access the weekly module area?

Well-Being

We have established that tertiary music classes (e.g., Bachelor of Music subjects) can be taught online as evidenced in research (Alcorn, 2018; Damon & Rockinson-Szapkiw, 2018; Eakes, 2009; Keast, 2009; Johnson et al., 2018). Furthermore, research in online learning upholds its resolve for effective learning structures of inclusive learning design, curriculum differentiation, as well as flexibility and access. Yet, prior to 2020, online music learning at the tertiary level in countries, like Australia, continues to be offered at a minimal level, if at all (Johnson & Cheok, in review). This is at a significantly lower rate when compared to over 40 per cent of American's National Association of Schools of Music (NASM) institutions offering online music classes in 2015 (Johnson, 2017).

Given the alarming challenge of student well-being is increasing (Baik, 2017) and the increasing concern of mental well-being of tertiary music students (Perkins et al., 2017), well-designed online music learning may be able to address music student well-being through online learning. However, there are a number of complexities to consider when teaching music. When looking to support student learning through online learning methods, it is important to understand the traditional models of teaching used in a discipline that address the authenticity of the discipline (Koh, 2017). That is, understanding the extent to which the online learning approach can support the necessary discipline-based learning outcomes. This is even more critical when a discipline has been traditionally taught in a master-apprentice approach.

Specifically, in music, the master-apprentice approach has allowed for students to have one-to-one time with the teacher so that acute nuances of technique and sound are attained. However, not all master-apprentice teaching outcomes are positive learning experiences as outlined by Hallam (1998). During music classes, students may be overwhelmed by the amount of material delivered at one time, experience language translation difficulties, or need the lesson to be approached from a different perspective. Each of these learning concerns contributes to the overall student well-being.

Therefore, given the corpus of research that suggests music students have particularly high levels of anxiety and need for preventative injury strategies, the lack surfacing of student well-being across the cases is concerning. For this reason, the framework specifically includes well-being as a component.

A considered approach to well-being requires the examination of student time on task, assessment format and time for completion of assessments, inclusion of community development within the online course itself, and instructor attention to student care. Each of these items can be addressed in the actual development and design of the course itself. Typically, curriculum guides outline the amount of overall semester time and weekly hours students should spend in class time and on assessments. Therefore, the instructor is responsible for ensuring that these timeframes are adhered to as well as including opportunities for student activities that develop community and supporting the student through regular virtual office hours and accessibility through email or other contact means.

Key Questions to Consider on Well-Being in Design

- What are explicit ways that you encourage student self-care?
- What is your institution's web page for student well-being?
- To what extent are you taking care of your own well-being in workload design?

Next Steps

Identifying online resources that will support effective student learning takes planning and preparation time. A planning resource list (see Chapter 9) may be a helpful tool to outline to ensure each online music course provides students with multiple ways to engage in their learning.

Questions for Personal Implementation

Key questions for the incorporation of specific aspects of design have been outlined above. Further design questions to reflect on include:

- To what extent have I focused on student engagement through design?
- How are course objectives resembled throughout the course structure?
- If I were a student, would I find my overall course easy to navigate?

5

Design: Case Studies

Introduction

The case studies, supported by research literature, underlined four key strategies for designing online music courses. Together, these strategies include organization, planning, accessibility, and well-being. It is noted that cases often had individual perspectives on how these strategies were developed and implemented in their online courses. One of the interesting outcomes from case studies was not only what was highlighted through the interviews and surveys, but also what appeared to be missing, or not addressed. This was the situation with regard to the topic of student well-being. Much of the data did not explicitly address how online music learning was designed and implemented to specifically support student well-being.

Faculty described specific and complex design processes that had to be completed in order to achieve an organized online course environment. These processes included the following actions: plan, create, and adjustment. While she thought about how one achieved meaningful online course design, one faculty member stated, 'It's really hard to tease all of this stuff out.' The culmination of initial course set up to online course creation required focused detail on lectures, reading notes, overall structured course content, and a need for advanced organizers and organization systems. The use of simple directions, easy-to-follow content and the use of targeted topics were helpful focus points to consider when designing online music courses. An iterative design process of plan, create, evaluate, and adjust was reiterated across the case studies.

Overall, the prominent design challenges were identified with regard to time management strategies for students and explorations to better manage the increased workload expected and required by instructors. Faculty acknowledged large amounts of time required in the preparation and planning and course creation stages. The amount of time given to pre-course workload was more than previously required for a face-to-face class. Challenges beyond planning the online course were noted to be the creation of multimedia content, seeking interactive online content, and identifying online activities that worked well for online learning environments. It was also noted that faculty spent an increased amount of time and workload responding to more email correspondence when teaching online. Students found themselves exploring new approaches to effectively manage their school time and instructors explored the use of music company's boxed course to provide a starting place in course design.

Finally, students found the online environment to support their musical skill development. Emphasizing how online music works for theory, electives an applied pedagogy, students appreciated and used the skills learned from one online class and across into the others. Overall purposeful course design was found to support the increase of music skill and enjoyment of the music learning process.

Case 1

As you likely recall from Chapter 1, Case One was a mid-sized university with a director (also an academic that taught classes), seven full-time music academics (including an administrator as lecturer), and fifty-two students in its music department. Focused on exploring technology and online classes for all subjects, the music department looked for instructors that were interested in implementing technology in their class. However, a majority (six out of seven) of the instructors were hired with little to no background in online teaching. Supported by university professional development workshops, instructors learned how to create online courses as required. Their diversity of teaching experiences ranged from little to no prior teaching or technology background to advanced technology users.

A unique aspect of this music programme was the use of hybrid, or dual-mode, teaching. While some students attended class on campus, other students attended class online from rural or neighbouring cities, as well as other countries. Aged eighteen to twenty-four years of age, students completed their degree requirements across four years.

Organization

Case One used a hybrid format[1] for teaching students. This meant all academic and instrumental classes were taught from an on-campus classroom, with online students participating in class through a synchronous video conference stream. If students were near the university, they had the option to attend weekly classes on-campus or via the synchronous live-stream.

From the interviews, one of the students expressed preference for the F2F learning environment as she perceived online students miss out on certain aspects of learning. She stated, 'I feel as if the online students don't get as much of a learning experience as the face-to-face students just because they don't.' The student also described how the hybrid course design accented the differences between the two student communities. She concluded '… I think that it would be a lot easier to take an online class if there was no F2F at all … I think that they should be separated.'

Careful preparation at the beginning was found to be part of the regular online course workload. A planning stage consisting of identification of course content and course resource to be made was apparent. Content creation required the majority of time in pre-course design. It was then followed by a stage of testing out of the course to 'make sure that everything works'.

Instructors also identified events or processes that highlighted problematic course design or content. For example, one instructor noted, 'If I keep getting emails about something, I recognize that it's probably a design flaw.' Furthermore, openness to adjustments in course design was found to be a reality in online teaching. The focus on 'rigorous but reasonable' course design was paramount.

The amount of work required of students in an online music course was determined by the faculty member designing the course. As noted by faculty, it was important to 'gaug[e] how much time an action takes in a class' and know the 'time restraints of the students' in your course. This included adding up the time for reading course materials, completing learning tasks, and participating in the live and recorded class times. During the faculty focus group discussion, this topic was highlighted as well. One faculty participant suggested faculty be realistic regarding how much time an average student takes to complete an assignment. For example, it was suggested that faculty should allot students one and a half times the length of a video for its assignment time. As a

---

[1] This mode of teaching is now often termed 'dual-mode' teaching.

comparison, another faculty member recalled how the face-to-face classroom allows for student 'pauses' in lesson time when a hand is raised. This notion of identifying a true sense of student's workload was deemed important for course design.

It was also suggested by a faculty member that there appear to be common errors which are committed when estimating workload. New online music faculty were described as [they] 'don't blink an eye at assigning students to read 40 or 50 pages for the next lecture. They forget that these are undergraduates they don't read as quickly or as thoroughly as we do.' One participant suggested it takes, '8 minutes to read a page'. From this it was observed that resources required for student reading and activity within the course workload need to be thought-out with regard to both time involved and diversity of activities/tasks.

All in all, student remarked that they appreciated clarity of organization and structures of course design. In particular, one student identified that the online structure assisted in showing her limited musical skill and knowledge because of purposeful course design. Furthermore, students identified that having the appropriate amount of work and technology were important considerations when designing a course.

Planning

Both faculty and students identified the importance of interactive course design on the impact of student engagement. For example, one aural skills instructor used active participation (e.g., singing during a synchronous session) and observed increased motivational student reaction to content. 'It is something that they get into,' he stated. 'It's something that they were singing, so they could look through the score and the score all of a sudden became life-like.' He further explained, 'My classes are never just like 100% lecture, that would be like really, really boring and they wouldn't get anything out of it.'

Dependent on familiarity of learning models and successful prior online learning tasks, faculty developed their course design accordingly. One faculty member described creating learning tasks by reflecting through the process of 'so what can you do on your computer that would be any way valuable?' Another faculty member identified 'too much stud [technology] is a turn off … and then they get so far away from what I'm actually teaching'. These divergent pedagogies in online course design were likely evidenced by students that commented, 'There was so many different online components, it was hard for … for me as a student to know what all [the instructor] wanted me to get done.'

Faculty identified that issues with course design could be reflected in the number of clarification emails instructors received from their students. Numerous questions regarding learning tasks, due dates, etc. could be identified as problematic design concerns. This notion was also raised in the faculty focus groups. Communicating with students was identified as possibility leading to design change, back to communicating with students, and then further design change – as iterative model. As one faculty member suggested in his interview, such questions suggest, 'It's a design issue and you need to go back and look at your design.' Overall, one faculty member confessed, 'I have to really learn how to explain something really well.' Students acknowledged that they could observe the differences in effective course design. One student expressed, 'I have two friends that were the same class, different instructors and a totally different experience.'

Reiterating the importance of music discipline knowledge, the faculty focus group participants expressed the importance of keeping the context of music learning and the apprenticeship model at the forefront of applied teaching, conducting, and skill-based classes. This viewpoint was again affirmed in two other faculty interviews.

One notable part of the process of course design included the creation of a backup plan. This plan ensured that if technology was limited, or didn't work, there is an alternate plan that provided students with the opportunity to continue in their weekly content learning and not be delayed into the semester.

Accessibility

With flexibility being one of the outcomes of online learning, instructors noted that the asynchronous recordings of lectures were not the most effective and interactive approach to learning. Specifically, a student remarked, 'The recording is fine … you can still watch what is going on, but you're not really included. You're just … watching.' This underscored the importance of overall course design to ensure that students had other opportunities for access to student engagement within the online class.

Well-Being

Parts of student well-being were explored through learning engagement. Instructors noted, 'The key is that there is transfer across the curriculum.' This pathway for student learning was described as a component that helped students 'from not really knowing anything about to making some, some rather educated and thoughtful responses about the music.' Therefore, learning engagement was found to be 'A realization of making sure that the class again is rigorous but that you're not giving students too much work to demonstrate learning.'

Faculty described a method of personalized coaching for their students in the online environment. Coaching was described as having more of a one-to-one connection between a faculty member and a student to help them learn a specific skill or understanding. One faculty member stated, 'My goal is mostly I need to get you to pass everything and what can we do in this timeframe.' Elaborating on what can happen during a coaching, faculty suggested, 'Usually we work on things that they need help with' as well as 'I have a piano right here and if I really need to, I say, "wait" and I just move my computer over there. And say, "watch my hands." This is what I'm doing.' Other faculty members described coaching students through conversations in email, during their weekly synchronous class sessions, and through asynchronous feedback.

The inclusion of flipped classroom techniques as part of online music teaching instruction was both familiar and being implemented in the online music course context with at least half of the faculty members. Faculty embedded this technique into their pedagogy as evidenced by one faculty who stated, 'I've been trying to do that [flipped classroom] more with them because I want to sit back and hear what they have to say and listen to them break it down because they'll find that they'll have the knowledge but they just have never put it to use.'

The flipped classroom was also identified as a means to create further student engagement in course content. 'We do that [flipped classroom] as well because I love the class participation and because they are going to be educators and performers and they have to be able to pull this off.'

Instructor Time Management

The subject of personal time management was described as 'the most difficult part of teaching online' by one music instructor. She then suggested how it is necessary to have discipline when responding to student email since it is first point of contact for online students.

Discussion from the faculty focus group also suggested there were perceived time limitations when comparing the desired time for student-instructor interaction to course load credit. An instructor further remarked, 'I'm working with them for a full half hour, to an hour each week with each student. And then, we'd be getting together for a one- or two-hour session where they can see each other and work together. That can happen with technology. It's very doable. But, when I'm getting two load credits to do this, it's just not feasible. It's not going to happen.' Another music instructor described his focused attention to online teaching as, 'I think it's easy to just get overwhelmed and always feel that there's something to do.' However, he admitted to creating healthy work boundaries and stated, 'I have to keep a time limit.'

Case 2

Positioned in a small music education department, a single music instructor, Instructor David (pseudonym), was given the task of teaching online music classes to both bachelor music students and music education students. With a broad background in the use of educational technology in music classes for over twenty years, David is an experienced innovator in online music teaching.

Organization

The use of organization was felt to be both a consideration of design and a necessary teaching tool for supporting student learning. He described the layout of a course as one that allowed students to experience a scaffolded approach to the learning content. He included a variety of asynchronous tools to ensure mono and bidirectional points of communication for learning. A focus on common and accessible tools in the course design ensured the support for Universal Design for Learning (UDL) which was also deemed to be paramount. These included: text, graphics, YouTube links for further explanations, and various LMS tools (e.g., drop box, discussion forums, email).

David described how it was important to provide thoughtful consideration as to when and how content was released during the semester. For example, students were able to move through asynchronous parts of the course through restricted release mechanisms in the LMS. Overall, he focused on modelling effective teaching in the online course area. The use of scaffolding and backward design was common strategies.

David stated that overall course design that focused on interaction was a key to online music learning. To reach that goal, community was built into the learning content and weekly activities. Using group projects, the instructor made sure that new students were able to become part of student membership quickly.

Within the course design, David limited the technology tools he used in order to keep curriculum at the forefront. He repeatedly stated that the focus of his courses was on content, not technology. To this end, David encouraged students to use technology that was common in their personal life. For example, he expected that students in the course could use YouTube and Google, as well as mobile device technology. He explicitly outlined the technology tool expectations in his syllabus.

Planning

To effectively situate his online teaching, David described how he spent time outlining, detailing, and building the course structure and layout such that students had opportunity to both learn independently and together in group activities. This learning design supported student achievement in assessment as well as sustained community across the semester.

He further described how he took time to identify any new technology tools that might be needed for student learning. Only one or two new technology tools were used in each course. In particular, the instructor built an app that supported the specific course content for the students. This allowed the students to access the course content in a mobile manner.

Accessibility

UDL was at the forefront of David's course design. His students were given opportunities to show what they know through different representations. For example, students were able to create video presentations, written scholarly works, create musical works of expression, etc. The focus was on ensuring that students attained the learning objectives and were able to engage in the content creatively.

Student Well-Being

To help support student well-being across the course, David repeatedly encouraged students to create support groups within the class and encouraged student-to-student video conference calls across the semester. By having a solid understanding of technology proficiency, he was also able to respond to minor technology issues for students.

David identified a high level of awareness, care, and time spent on his online material preparation. This further supports the importance of allocating an adequate amount of focused time to prepare online materials in advance.

Case 3

In case study three, there were six instructors and five students that took part in surveys, interviews, and focus groups. Offering a variety of bachelor music degrees in graduate programmes, students took part in online classes from multiple campuses and locations. Technology was a core component of the university programme, with each undergraduate required to complete the first-year technology course. A suite of four online music courses was offered each semester in the areas of musicology (i.e., popular music and world music) as well as music theory. All online music courses required the students to complete the course content and assignments through the LMS. Online course design at this institution did not use synchronous or live, video conference streaming. Online learning took place in an asynchronous manner.

Organization

The approach to teaching music online relied on the unique previous teaching experiences of each instructor. While each instructor was identified as having interest in technology and the use of technology in teaching music, all instructors in this case study found themselves seeking external support to learn how to plan and organize for their first teaching of an online music course. Overall, the institutional support of workshops was found limited towards the understanding of supporting online music teaching. As such, many of the online music instructors found themselves sharing their organization and planning strategies with each other to help form effective design approaches.

One of the challenges to class organization was the overall organization of the class itself. For example, some instructors chose to organize their classes with focused student interaction that unfolded each week across the full semester, whereas other instructors chose an asynchronous, non-timed approach (i.e., content and activities could be completed any time before the last day of semester). It was noted by the different instructors that students were uncertain about how their online course would take place across the semester due to the mixed approaches of both synchronous and asynchronous approaches used with the department. This uncertainty not only created student questions about class organization but was perceived by instructors as a non-unified structure that could potentially undermine overall student learning.

Organization Clarity

Clarity was found to be a term used to describe content organization. It encompassed both the online course structure itself (e.g., the use of weekly modules, web pages, document resources) and the connection of content to multimedia (i.e., video, audio, and graphic representations). Overall, planning was the practical action of identifying *how* the faculty member achieved the organization.

Technology Processes

Course design also had specific challenges directly due to technology. One online music instructor expressed a concern for the level of faculty learning about new technologies and how that can sometimes affect grading. She explained that if an online quiz were created with the wrong response indicated as right in the LMS, the correct answer would appear as a wrong response causing a loss of quiz point(s). Awareness of the possible challenges that could come with technology innovation was part of the solution for both faculty and students alike.

One of the notable scaffolds was the need for students to have familiarity with general knowledge of technology. To aid this familiarity, students were required to complete computer proficiency courses in their general education requirements. This allowed students to have familiarity with the learning management system, and basic multimedia creation, which help to alleviate the need for instructors to support students with technology help.

Planning

The planning and creation of the online classes required focus time for each instructor. In general, faculty members found they had to 'transition' their teaching and be able to adapt and change their course design for the online music learning environment. Previous on-campus classroom activities and their corresponding activities were found untranslatable to the online environment. This meant that instructors had to spend time re-conceptualizing how content could be effectively explored in an online class. Taking time to actively plan and transform teaching to an online pedagogy, instructors described their workload including editing lectures and content into concise and 'succinct' briefings. Feelings of being time poor, such as 'I really wish that I would have had more time to prepare, to implement the course', were expressed.

To counter the preparation time for designing a new online class, one instructor used a prefabricated online music course. To better align the course to content and activities that were more appropriate for her student body, one instructor found herself adapting and altering the boxed course design. 'What [boxed course software] gives me is not exactly what I want.' Consequently, she used student feedback to continue to adjust and improve her course. Another instructor remarked that the boxed course content was 'technically' correct. 'But there's no way it can stay that way. It's got to be improved upon.'

New to teaching music online, one instructor found herself reaching out to colleagues at other institutions for advice on developing an effective plan. She found advice from her colleagues helpful for setting up her initial online course. Through her advance planning, she was able to identify organizational practices that would support her students' learning (e.g., inclusion of presentations, video, and weekly interactive discussion forums). She also found specific planning techniques were helpful supports during the semester. These included an introductory email sent out to all students prior to class starting that explained 'this is how the class is organized and this is where you will find the class material'. Echoed by multiple instructors, the sending of the introductory email provided students with clarity of expectations and semester planning that had positive implications across the teaching semester.

Using the comparison of her traditional face-to-face music class, a musicology instructor stated, 'What I do in person is that I try to do more of that scaffolding where we learn that language and then we continue that thread throughout all the other units.' Finding the boxed course lacking in all the necessary terminology and personalized order of learning scaffolds, she implemented a redesign that supported her established teaching scaffolds.

Overall, the planning of course design involved a process that included a cycle of plan, create, and adjust. While faculty members chose to allocate their time differently to each part of this cycle, some form of this cycle was evident through all faculty member interviews across the cases. Data from Case One emphasized an over-arching course design process while Case Three identified this cycle through a process of re-design due to its inclusion of 'boxed' courses.

Accessibility

The availability of accessibility for all online music faculty to enter into a learning process, regardless of technology background or teaching experience, was essential for both participants. In the focus group, one discussant defined accessibility as 'a way to sort of draw all people towards the goal, regardless of their age, inexperience or direction in education … drawing people to the same level playing field immediately so that you see there's an entry point for me.' The discussants understood the cyclical movement from each component. From the interactive discussion, it was agreed by the participants that there needs to be accessibility for all students to join in, and therefore, any framework must be both accessible and intuitive.

All faculty members interviewed in Case Three highlighted students taking the online music courses due to the flexible nature of off-campus studies. Citing, 'It's something they can do at their own pace, they don't have to worry about showing up,' instructors described students' affinity for its flexibility. Often using a single weekly discussion format, instructors describe students completing their course content items within a self-devised time frame.

Well-Being

Because of the nature of the 'boxed' course design, faculty members described how some of their students worked ahead of the calendar due dates. One instructor remarked, 'I don't know if that's [course work completion] a good or bad thing yet, but the ones that have done that are doing very well.' She reiterated the fact that students desiring flexibility of the online course design were able to move forward in their motivation to complete course content within a time frame that was pleasing to their schedule. She further explained, 'The only things they can't do ahead of time are the discussion forums, and the mid-term and the final,' which allowed for students to continue interacting with their course peers.

Overall, many of the instructors identified the need of increased hours given when constructing an online music course. One instructor identified that her administration provided her with course leave in order to develop her online music course. However, this was not identified across all instructors. Focused time for instructor self-care and time management strategies were highlighted in the interviews. However, instructors noted that there was not administrative understanding of the degree to which their workload increased when teaching online. This was found to be a well-being issue that had yet to be resolved.

Questions to Consider

Key aspects for design across all cases included careful content organization and meaningful approaches to instructor planning. Given the large time periods required to plan and organize the content, instructors developed their courses prior to the start of this semester.

- Given the need for detailed planning, what might be some strengths and weaknesses you foresee when you begin designing your online music course?
- What are helpful organizers that can support your course design?
- To what extent do you foresee course design to be challenging?

6

Assessment

Research Context

Assessment can be an opportunity for creativity as well as function in an online music class; this is also possible in the face-to-face classroom. However, both formats require a careful balance to ensure that the assessment is doing what it needs to do: provide evidence of the learning and skills attained by the student.

The oft-raised controversy of developing assessment activities and tasks for the online music class centre can be categorized around two focal points: realistic assessment and technology use. As found in many conservatories and music schools, some music instructors have raised the issue that while the online environment may be sufficient for submitting written papers or giving presentations, it does not provide students with a realistic experience for learning and demonstrating music performance skills (Johnson, 2017). Instructors may feel that the level of technology skill needed for students to take part in online music assessments (e.g., record a music performance or presentation) is outside the scope of skills required in the field of music. These challenges to online music assessment can be valid; however, it requires further exploration as to the integrity of the foundational argument upon which both of these aspects are positioned: authenticity.

Key Framework Components

This chapter will highlight the key component of assessment through four strategies that are supported in the literature and from the case studies: authentic to discipline, assessment design individual and group assessment, and feedback in assessment (see Figure 6).

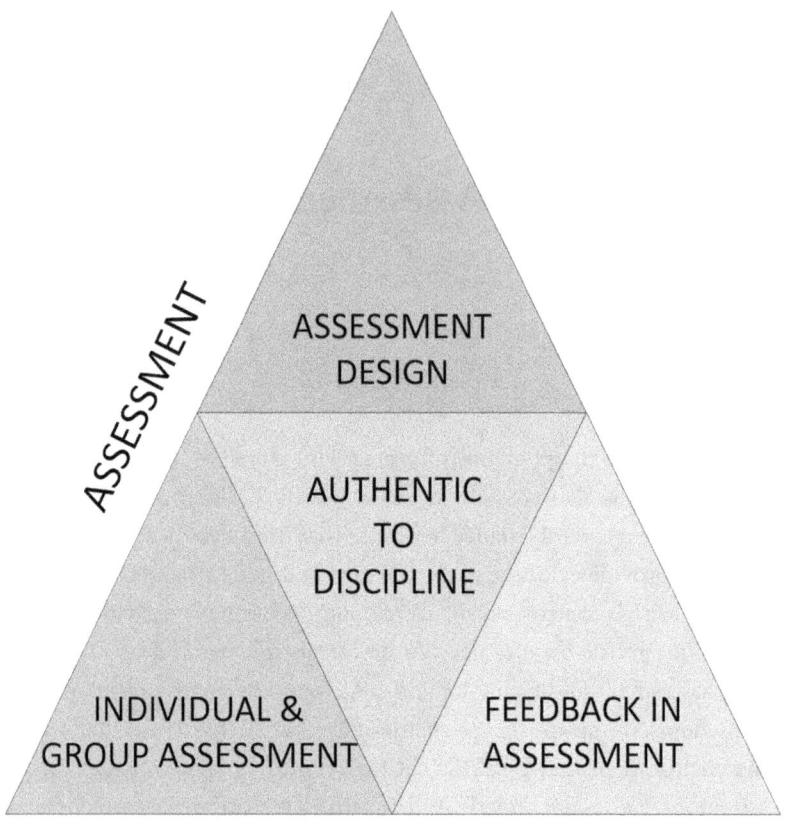

Figure 6 Assessment Component of Framework for Teaching Music Online.

Authentic to Discipline

There is a central focus that impacts multiple aspects of assessment: Authenticity. Authenticity is key for all aspects of assessment in all disciplines and in all forms of teaching modes (Koh, 2017). In terms of music as art, it becomes even more critical to address authenticity as the perception of music itself is tied to one's belief and values (i.e., ontological premise) and is present within a group's, school's, and society's cultural understanding. Given the paucity of research currently available on the authenticity of online music assessment, one should be mindful of the need to continue to keep abreast of new research that becomes available. Currently, it is understood that authenticity can be attained in online music assessment, albeit in approaches that have similarities and differences to face-to-face assessment approaches. Ultimately, before choosing any assessment activity, we first must ensure that the assessment is authentic to the discipline of music.

A key reference to authentic assessment is found in the work of Koh (2017). Compiling and categorizing seminal works, Koh's *Criteria for Authenticity in Authentic Assessment* outlines eight components that can support the evaluation of an assessment with regard to authentic assessment. These components, as outlined by Koh, are:

1. Real-world relevance
2. Application of skill transferability in new contexts
3. Discipline-specific; Deep learning
4. Practical experiential opportunities and receive instructor feedback
5. Multiple evidence over time
6. Transparent and explicit scoring system
7. Self-assessment woven in
8. Evidence of reliability for scoring outcome

Each of these components will be examined and exemplified in the following section to aid in situating key questions that instructors can ask themselves to evaluate the degree of authenticity of an online music assessment.

As we look to authenticity through real-world relevance (Koh, 2017), an online music assessment should embody an activity or outcome that the student would encounter in a future music position, or career. For example, if an online assessment requires a student to record an ensemble part to an online recording software (e.g., Soundtrap.com or Bandcamp.com) production track, one must ask if in the future a student would encounter the need to have knowledge and skills in performance recording. Given that graduating students may need to create an audition recording or band recording, such an assessment could be deemed authentic, provided it meets a majority of the other criteria. A key question for examining real-world relevance of an online music assessment is: To what extent would a musician need the skills attained in this activity for future music performance or music teaching?

Koh's (2017) second criterion highlights the need for an assessment to support trans-disciplinary skills in new contexts. Evidencing thinking tools of trans-disciplinary skill acquisition and application, Root-Bernstein and Root-Bernstein (1999) identify trans-disciplinary skills (i.e., abstracting, perceiving, observing, and patterning among others) that can be linked to achieving and evidencing creativity (Henriksen et al., 2014). These skills are used not only in a single discipline such as music but are thinking tools that can be used in other disciplines. Musicians are often identified as having a diverse skill set (Johnson et al., 2020) and use their skills attained in music to flourish inside and beyond music-specific careers. Therefore, the online music instructor should examine and evaluate each assessment for the appropriateness of connection to trans-disciplinarity. For example, a student may not initially be familiar with using a particular video recording software or application as a student; however, perhaps she often records personal videos for friends. Providing transferability of technology tool application through abstracting (e.g., what else can this technology tool be used to create) supports trans-disciplinarity of skill for new contexts. A key question specific to addressing the criteria of trans-disciplinary skills is: What, if any, are the transdisciplinary skills obtained from this assessment?

When we think of deep learning in authentic assessment (Koh, 2017), we are going beyond 'surface learning' (Biggs, 1999). Deep learning (Biggs, 1999; Scott, 2006) is established by critically examining new and previous knowledge and skills and bridging these ideas together in a meaningful manner. For example, one could transform a 250-word discussion post into a deep-learning activity provided that the question requires meta-cognitive thinking. That is, a student should move through self-reflection (e.g., what did I do in the past), to meta-cognitive thinking (e.g., what can I change to do things differently in the future). A key question to ensure authenticity of deep learning is: To what extent is there opportunity for the student to reflect and take up new ideas for the future?

In music teaching, we often incorporate performance opportunities and overt practical opportunities in our assessments. However, authenticity of assessment also requires an action of instructor feedback (Koh, 2017). This means that the instructor provides the student with timely feedback in a manner that is appropriate to the assessment. For example, a written paper in the middle of semester may have more formative instructive feedback than a final paper positioned at the end of the semester. Both assessments require the instructor to elucidate opportunities, strengths, and challenges found within the writing to ensure the student has opportunity for feed-forward and feed-up (see section on Feedback) application. A key question to support authenticity of instructor feedback is: When will students receive timely feedback on the assessment and to what degree will the feedback provide new strategies for future?

The criterion of multiple evidence of assessment (Koh, 2017) can be challenging to instructor workload if advance planning has not taken place. Multiple assessments provide the student with opportunities to show a scaffolded learning development across a particular time or semester.

Evidence of learning can be formal (i.e., graded) and informal (i.e., non-graded). For example, students may have the opportunity to perform at various online recitals during the semester wherein the instructor provides brief feedback along with vetted 'critical friend feedback' from other students in the class. A key question to consider with regard to authenticity is: To what extent does the student have opportunity to demonstrate achievement of assessment across a period of time?

The use of a transparent and explicit scoring system in authentic assessment (Koh, 2017) provides online students with clarity and decreased anxiety over assignment expectations. Online assessments and their accompanying rubrics or scoring criteria are often clarified multiple times by the online instructor due to the limited interaction with a student outside of class. Whereas an on-campus student may have an informal hallway conversation with an instructor, the online student may reach out via email for clarity. For example, transparency can be supported by highlighting the location of a rubric and/or briefly examining the rubric during an online class or via LMS announcement. A key question to ask regarding transparency of scoring system is: Where can the student locate the key criteria or rubric for the assessment?

Identified extensively across music learning research, self-assessment as self-regulation is a general practice strategy used by musicians (McPherson & Zimmerman, 2011; Nielsen, 2004; Zimmerman, 2011b). Skills such as self-monitoring, error correction, and deliberate practice are common traits exhibited by musicians in their practice (Eriksson, 1997; Meinz & Hambrick, 2010). There are many ways to incorporate the use of self-reflection in a music assessment. For example, the use of checklists, discussions on performance practice, and the direct highlight of a rubric can support opportunities for self-assessment. One key question to determine self-assessment supports within an assessment is: To what extent is the self-assessment support hidden or overt in the assessment?

The final criteria, evidenced of reliability of scoring outcome, provides opportunity for the student, and others where warranted, the links between the achievement level and score, or grade. That is, an authentic assessment in music will be appropriately scored in terms of the expectation of the music performance and music education disciplines. This is an opportunity for students to understand what level of achievement is expected in the practice of the discipline. For example, in the online music class, these criteria may be effectively evidenced by the instructor performing the corrected musical interpretation of the music or highlighting a current research debate on a topic.

Connected to the real-world criteria, a key question to highlight this criterion is: To what extent is the student score aligned to current music practices or music performance?

When implementing authenticity in assessment, one should consider how the objective in a real-world music performance or music career scenario. This exploration, along with addressing each of the eight authenticity components, will aid in ensuring that the assessment aligns to authenticity in the discipline.

Questions to Consider for Authenticity in Assessment

- What is the real-life activity that this assessment activity is mirroring?
- What are key activities that all music students should be prepared to encounter in their music careers?
- To what extent will certain technology skills be required by these music students in their future careers?; How does each assessment help support that need for authentic technological knowledge?

Assessment Design

In assessment design, there are two basic types of assessment approaches to identify students' knowledge and skill level: summative and formative assessment. In brief, summative assessments are generally ones that are finite (e.g., performance recital) and attached with a single final grade. The summative assessment is often associated with the final exam of a topic unit or, end of semester project. Formative assessments focus on the notion of continued development of learning and are used as an assessment that allows for feedback to be given to the student. This feedback is then incorporated into the assessment for continued improvement and development across the assessment. This means that there can be multiple feedback loops that provide the student with opportunity to further develop the learning outcomes while in moving forward to complete a larger objective. In his work on constructive alignment in teaching, Biggs (2003) outlines four steps for designing assessment in learning: '1. Defining the intended learning outcomes (ILOs); 2. Choosing teaching/learning activities likely to lead to the ILOs; 3. Assessing students' actual learning outcomes to see how well they match what was intended; 4. Arriving at a final grade' (Biggs, 2003, p. 2).

Summative assessments for online music classes can include the submission of written papers, vocabulary quizzes, listening exams, podcast and websites, recorded video performances and recitals, and various forms of final projects. Each of these assessment activities are of themselves a complete form of assessment (i.e., culminate in a grade).

On the other hand, formative online music assessments are often found as longer term activities and may include: mid-semester performance videos, submission of an outline prior to the final written paper, vocabulary and listening mastery quizzes, and post-and-reply discussion forum activities. Formative assessment may also include informal, non-graded formative assessments such as in-class or forum-based discussions, student-and-instructor email threads or a synchronous video chat, student-to-student review of weekly music performances, peer commentary on mid-semester performances, and peer review of draft- or completed-projects.

Planning Assessments

As supported by Biggs' (2003) assessment process addressed above, assessment is a mechanism to demonstrate current attainment of specific class objectives (e.g., a recorded performance) and provide opportunity to give individual student feedback. In the online space, assessment needs to be carefully planned – due to the nature of the visual course design – and crafted to line up with the module or weekly design of the online course.

Constructive alignment of learning (Biggs, 2003) supports that idea that planning for assessments cannot take place before learning objectives for a course have been realised. This means that course planning or the course timeline needs to identified before the assessments are created – the learning objectives are the focus points for all aspects of course design. Projects can be scaffolded into multiple parts so that a formative assessment process can better support the final learning outcome. For example, a 3000-word research essay maybe a final outcome, yet it can be supported with an initial outline assessment do earlier in the semester. This type of multi-part formative assessment allows for the instructor, or tutor, to provide feedback to the student on the research outline. The student then can use the instructor feedback to influence a stronger final research paper – this creates a feedback loop.

Formative assessments can also be part of music performance learning. For example, a student may have a mid-semester recital wherein students provide critical commentary (i.e., peer review) to a video of the recitalist's performance or dress rehearsal. This type of formative peer feedback allows for both the recitalist and the students-as-audience to encounter learning from multiple points-of-view. Also, this type of formative assessment helps to support students in developing critical feedback skills as they carefully craft feedback comments when observing their peers perform.

The important aspects to consider when planning assessments are the timing of the assessment within the semester, coordination of other large assessments across the degree programme, and ensuring the assignments are directly linked to the course objectives (see Johnson (2018) for linking assessments and course objectives).

Examples of Academic Activities to Consider:

- Research papers
- Website/Blog
- Cumulative Project
- Podcast
- Evaluate a Podcast
- Graduate Journal Publication
- Video Presentation
- Concert Programme Notes
- Journalistic Interview
- Research Pilot

Special Populations

As mentioned earlier, all students are unique learners, and the online environment may or may not provide the most effective learning environment for every learner. Given that the online environment can provide additional supportive forms of learning that provides flexibility (e.g., asynchronous activities) and accessibility (e.g., non-co-located learning), online music classes may be opportune for special populations to study music performance. Assessments that provide differentiation and inclusive forms of assessment should be considered (Colwell et al., 2017). For example, an assessment may provide students with an option to complete an individual project or a group project, if aligned with the course objectives. Further, an assessment should be reasonably approachable for students experiencing limited sight, vision, cognition, and motor skills.

Questions to Consider for Authenticity in Assessment

Authenticity in Assessments ensures assessments not only provide students with active and participatory experiences, and that these activities are relevant to the music discipline in various ways. The following questions can help support authenticity in assessment:

- How is this assessment related to the real-world work of musicians?
- To what extent can the activity be separated into manageable segments, or parts, that can provide students with opportunities to experience the assessment from multiple points of view?
- How can students show their knowledge in multiple ways, yet still address the main content achievement of the assessment criteria?
- To what extent does the assessment address the class objectives?

Individual and Group Assessment

Exploring the opportunities of individual and group music lessons, Mitchell (2020b) highlights the importance that both forms of learning provide for students. Each learning experience allows this student to engage in activities that require different skills. For example, an individual assessment provides evidence of the student's ability for solo performance, individual listening skills, and individual activity management whereas a group assessment allows all students to demonstrate their collaborative skills and cooperation with others. Sharing of knowledge and communication skills are further explored in group assessments. While Mitchell considers the use of group music performance lessons, this research also has implications for group music assessment.

If we consider the key important mechanisms of self-reflection and self-regulation in music, we can see that individual assessment can be part of important steps in musical learning. The creation of musician as self-assessor and self-reflector is central. However, music is often created in collaboration. Therefore, providing students with the opportunity to experience similar real world group performance requires the use of group assessment.

A useful approach for supporting positive group assessment outcomes is the sharing and development of group membership expectations. While some instructors may have prefabricated group membership expectation criteria,

Table 1 Examples of Individual and Group Online Assessment Activities.

Individual Assessment Activities	Group Assessment Activities
Video of Performance Recital	Live-Streamed Individual Recitals as Concerts
Weekly Video Performance Journal/Diary	Virtual Reality Performances
Peer Review of Student Performances using Discussion Board	Ensemble Recording Project using Recording Application (e.g., Soundtrap.com)
Self-Reflection Activity on Practice Outcomes	Live-Streamed Student Teaching Demonstration

providing students with an opportunity to add or enrich the criteria through student voice can be helpful. Table 1 provides some ideas to consider for online activities.

Feedback in Assessment

As music instructors, one of the keys to effective assessment is being an expert in our music discipline. With discipline expertise, we should be able to identify the graduated levels and skillsets of the required disciplinary performance and knowledge and be able to assess what level of skill and knowledge each student has attained. Given the nature of music as art, assessing aspects of musicianship and music performance is a challenging task. However, with pre-established class objectives (see Chapter 6 Design), the development and implementation of assessment can be both a rigorous and rewarding learning experience for both students and instructors.

While both summative and formative assessment can have graded outcomes, research underscores how formative assessment can support students in a more cyclical development for learning (Black & Wiliam, 1998). In general, this cyclical development provides students with opportunity to receive feedback on their learning from the instructor. Feedback is an important part in the assessment learning cycle. In the hands of an effective instructor, feedback can be used to help a student 'confirm, add to, overwrite, tune, or restructure information in memory, whether that information is domain knowledge, meta-cognitive knowledge, beliefs about self and tasks, or cognitive tactics and strategies' (Winne & Butler, 1994, p. 5740). From the standpoint of the student-as-recipient, feedback can be used in three ways: as **feed*back*** that prompts a reflective review and self-reflection

(Biggs, 2003; Hattie & Timperley, 2007); as a **feed-*forward*** (Hattie & Timperley, 2007; Quinton & Smallbone, 2010) revision tool that supports engagement with the feedback for future; and as **feed-*up*** (a process that supports change of practice through self-regulation). While instructors are often more familiar with feedback, the formation and development of teaching design to situate students well to embrace and transition feedback to their feed-forward and feed-up counterparts is situated in the *Framework* as part of both assessment and design.

Visually demonstrating the importance of feedback in teaching, consider Figure 7. Starting from the left side of the graph, we can see how increased amounts of open feedback dialogue (i.e., dialogue that supports feed-forward and feed-up actions) and increased autonomy in activities corresponds to increased motivation. This suggests that with a strong, and intuitive online learning design, and clarity of assessment purpose, students will perceive a decrease in frustration.

Feedback can occur during along the learning cycle itself as is common in formative assessments. Formative assessments are graded activities that provide the student with opportunities to learn across the assessment process. For

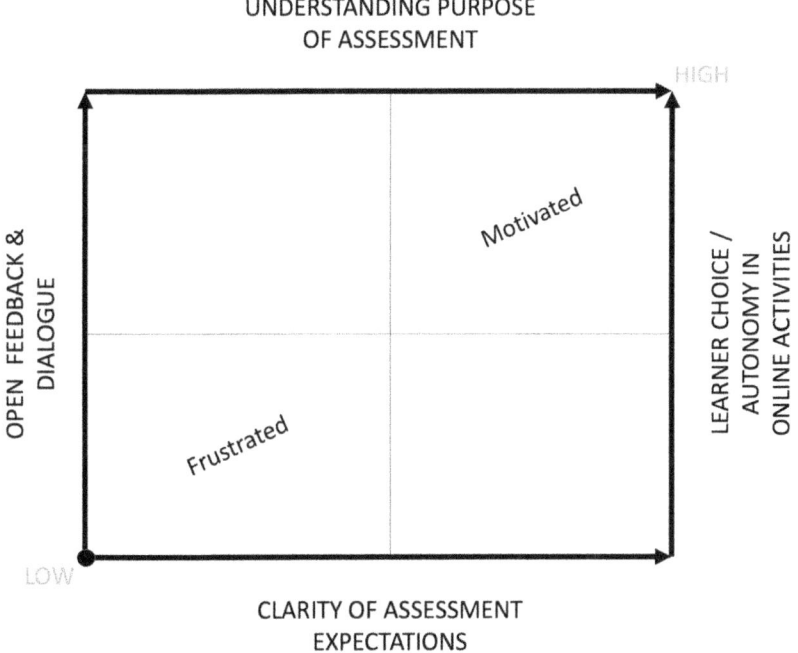

Figure 7 Creating Student Motivation through Assessment Design Using Feedback and Learner Autonomy.

DESIGN ORGANIZER FOR ONLINE COURSE DESIGN

	Week 1	Week 2	Week 3	Week 7	Week 11	Week 12
Learning content	Introduction to Saxophone Pedagogy	Exploring pedagogical approaches (share masterclass videos)	Lesson Planning	Teaching Demo #1	Teaching Demo #2	Reflections on Personal Saxophone Pedagogy
Assessment	Individual: Student to locate one international pedagogue masterclass video	Individual: Students to evaluate pedagogy according to framework in class	Group: Students to collate different lesson planning templates	Individual: Student demonstrates a 20-minute lesson Group: Critical Friend Peer Review	Individual: Student demonstrates a 20-minute lesson	Pedagogy Research Project

Figure 8 Scaffolding of Projects to a Final Project.

example, this may mean that an assessment is scaffolded into various multiple projects that then cumulatively lead towards more complex projects, and a final project (see Figure 8).

During the formative assessment process, there is opportunity for the instructor to provide formal feedback (e.g., a grade; instructor comments in a rubric) and informal feedback (e.g., email conversations, Zoom chats, and peer review) that the student can use to improve their learning. Further, as in the example shown in Figure 13, students are able to provide peer feedback through an activity of 'Critical Friend' feedback. In this activity, students watch as individual student demonstration and provide specific comments on the 'performance.' It should be noted that providing examples of effective critical friend feedback is an important initial set-up to the activity.

The following outline examples of feedback, feed-forward and feed-up in action.

Ways for students to receive feedback include:

- instructor provides asynchronous text-based, or video feedback;
- instructor provides informal synchronous discussion;
- keeping a journal/diary of class or practice routine;
- writing a reflective essay;
- students watching video recording of their performances;

- students observing music performance masterclasses from YouTube;
- critical friend activities (e.g., students providing peer review on a peer's video performance).

Activities demonstrating feed-forward process:

- assessment contains multiple parts for students to scaffold learning into assessments;
- students using teacher feedback to revise a specific performance or project idea;
- students changing a targeted aspect of their performance or music teaching due to self-reflection activity;
- student using identified peer remarks to change an observed behaviour or response

Evidence of feed-up activities:

- a student has adapted a new practice routine and is sharing that routine with others;
- a student has overcome a knowledge gap in teaching and is using the new knowledge when conducting an ensemble.

In his book on maximizing student learning, John Hattie (2012) highlights four levels of feedback: *Task and Product Level, Process Level, Self-Regulation or Conditional Level, and Self Level*. Part of a larger interconnected matrix, the multiple levels of feedback are themselves supports that assist students in understanding the successfulness of current progress, understanding their next phase of learning to attain, and suggesting how to proceed. As noted by Hattie, most feedback given to students is in the form of the correct/incorrect nature of Task and Produce Level feedback. Process Level feedback positively supports students to advance beyond their current achievement level as it highlights more than surface ideas to suggest strategies and approaches that ask students to explore deeper knowledge. This in turn promotes self-efficacy in the student. The third feedback level, Self-Regulation, focuses on student reflection; this form of feedback prompts self-regulation skills in student and offers the student further questions for self-examination. The final level, Self, is one wherein the feedback is focused on the student themselves and not related to the activity of the task. Related to instructor choice and desired outcome, these feedback approaches are used interchangeably, as well as given in tandem.

To Give Praise, or Not?

Noted in much of the literature on feedback, the well-intentioned feedback of mere adulation, termed Self Level feedback by Hattie (2012), often does not spur the student on towards deeper learning. It may surprise us to know that showering a student with glowing praise on an assignment doesn't extend student learning. However, this lack of engagement is often due to the nature of the praise statement – it is likely in the form of an unfocused and untethered statement (e.g., 'good job!'). According to Hyland and Hyland (2001), the lack of clarity from such written praise statements can ultimately diminish student motivation for future engagement.

While we do not set out to side-line students because of a praise statement, better engagement can be achieved when positive feedback is tethered to a specific portion of an assignment or performance and clearly articulated. However, such qualified statements can lead to extended written feedback and increased time and workload. Therefore, the need for clarification suggests an exploration for non-text feedback that can better assist students in understanding what needs to be improved and how this can be taken up in the future.

Supporting Learning with Video Feedback

As mentioned earlier, there are aspects of on-campus learning that can also support an online class. The use of multimedia, as an asynchronous learning support, is an effective tool for online assessment as instructors can use it to effectively convey teacher feedback for student learning (Borup et al., 2015).

Based on the theory of Universal Design for Learning (UDL) as described by Meyer et al. (2014), multimedia provides students with opportunities to see, hear, and experience feedback in ways that can create a connected experience for students. Rising above the challenges of vague commenting or unclear written feedback, multimedia weaves together pictures with audio to provide support simultaneous cognitive and affective knowledge connections (Mayer, et al., 2014).

Multimedia can be used as a vehicle to highlight instructor feedback to a student. In this approach, the student experiences feedback through sight and sound, and feedback from the instructor's voice itself. That is, the instructor's voice inflections help provide another mechanism to assist the student in decoding feedback for clarity of idea and feedforward applications. In a commented paper, as student may see a highlighted paragraph, or commented sentence. Depending on the previous experiences of the student, the highlighting or comment can be interpreted in multiple ways. However, when a voice speaks the comment, there is the additional layer of voice inflection that supports further interpretation of visual and text message provided. For example, a voice inflection could suggest urgency, or emphasize importance of the comment. There can be problematic interpretations from brief, text-based feedback statements (e.g., 'Grammar issue', 'Need to clarify', 'Unclear statement'). However, a voice stating the same words can elucidate clarity through tone of voice. As a result, instead of a student incorrectly interpreting text-based feedback as negative feedback, the instructor's voice in the video underscores support and care.

In a qualitative review, Killingback et al. (2019) synthesized 450 higher education research studies to elucidate further understanding of non-text-based forms of instructor feedback. In their search, ten research studies met their key criteria for alternative forms of feedback (e.g., audio, screencasts, podcasts) for assessment. Thematic analyses of the studies suggest that these types of feedback mechanisms can be a rich resource and support for student learning. The five themes include: 'belonging, greater comprehension from non-verbal aspects of communication, individualized and personal, technical/practical technology aspects, and circumstances' (p. 34). Various noted studies (Ice et al., 2007; Marriott & Teoh, 2012; McSwiggan & Campbell, 2017) suggested that the use of audio provided students with a form of affective connection that positioned the feedback to be more helpful and receptive to students overall. This aspect of affective connection through sound is of particular importance for music students since musicians spend their careers focusing on the detail and interpretation of sound.

From this perspective, using video in music performance learning in the on-campus structure can also be an authentic learning connection. That is, feedback that contains music in its visually notated form and as an auditory sound, can be a way for students to further connect and interpret music notation and lexicon to specific sounds as well as musical symbols.

Describing musical terms in an online text-based format would not be an authentic depiction of music itself since it is a sound-based art form. This means that providing text-based comments as feedback may not be most effective for learning. For example, if a student submits video recital performance online, often it is helpful for the student to have immediate feedback. If the feedback is given more than 30 minutes after the assessment experience, the feedback may not be as meaningful to the student since the event or recital has lapsed in time and memory. Therefore, if there is a video used as feedback in tandem with formative assessment (i.e., verbal feedback), instructors can play the different parts of the recital or sing / vocalise different aspects that can provide audio as well as video. This also means that specific issues of posture, instrument position and articulation can be made more explicit with the use of audio and video feedback for students.

Video Feedback in Online Learning for Music Performance

Research highlights the use of video feedback as useful for blended and online delivery modes as well as on-campus learning. The value of video in learning is exemplified in the use of synchronous video exchanges (Bower et al., 2015), asynchronous communications (An & Lim, 2009; Vonderwell, 2003), and as stand-along feedback mechanisms. When investigating the outcome of video use in student learning, it is evident that it is not the use of video alone that produces meaningful learning for students. Borup et al. (2015) highlight the use of three key elements for feedback quality in relation to effective communication through use of video and audio: content and utility; timing and efficiency; and delivery and affective support (p. 163). Specifically, this means that the intentional focus of *what, how, and when* content is addressed is of particular importance to students and their receptivity to the feedback. With practice, video can be used to convey feedback to a student that can, in turn, model expectations and learning strategies that further support student learning.

An example of online video feedback is found in a study by Johnson and Lock (2018), where the use of online video feedback for a student assignment was found by students to support personal learning connections between the student and instructor. One student in the cohort study remarked 'the last feedback that [instructor] did fantastic. I could look at my article and at a specific point, she was talking about what needed to be done, when she had the pointer, and absolutely great. Really, really helped my learning' (p. 1545). The inclusion of video feedback provided the student with purposeful context that prompted clarity of understanding. Given the limited connection that some students can feel in the online environment, taking up teaching approaches that position students for certainty of understanding through provision of unequivocal communication is key.

Questions to Consider on Feedback in Assessment

- To what extent should the assessment opportunities include self-reflection and/or peer review activities?
- Approximately how many formal and informal group work activities does the student encounter within the semester? Should there be more? Should there be less?
- How is transparency of instructor feedback addressed in the class?
- How effective is the instructor feedback?
- To what extent is feedback provided in text, video and audio formats?

Examples of Assessment Activities

There are various ways to assess music performance and academic skills in the online environment. Some of these approaches were mentioned earlier in the chapter.

Video Journals

One of the helpful activities that embrace video for student learning are video journals. During a performance class semester, students can be asked to submit a video journal activity once per week or every fortnight. The student can create a short, three-minute video that highlights their current performance ability, skills, and knowledge, as well as challenges. For example, a student could perform for two minutes in the video which is then preceded by one minute of verbal responses to specific learning questions as created by the teacher. Questions like, 'what is an area that you are having most challenges with this week?' Or, 'identify two or three musicians or ensembles that you listen to this week.' The use of specific questions for students to answer highlights expected activities that students should be addressing each week. This type of questioning also helps support students to learn helpful reflective questions and further their overall self-regulation skills. Encouraging the students to listen to their own video prior to submitting the recording journal also supports further student reflection.

Instructor Video Responses

Students can understand the effectiveness of hearing and seeing video content through a video response by the teacher. If the instructor uses video response to the student's video journal, students often remark on how effective and efficient it is for improving practice. Students can watch the asynchronous video at a convenient and flexible time as well as re-watch and pause the video to carefully take in the instructor's feedback and suggestions. Demonstration of posture, instrument technique, breath support, and a myriad of other key skills and components can be shared by the instructor to the student through a video response.

Further Online Assessment Tools to Consider

- **Individual self-assessment feedback mechanisms for online music teaching**
  - Student checklists
  - Calendaring
  - Video journals

- **Student-to-student feedback mechanisms**
  - Purpose
  - Key: Model mechanism, student self-assessment (where possible), then student-to-student approach
    - Discussion boards
    - Video analyses of performances
    - Peer review of papers prior to submission

Alternate Assessment

Alternate assessment is the reframing of an assessment for special populations (Colwell et al., 2017) or extraordinary teaching and learning circumstances. Both alternatives require that the assessment provide the student with an assessment that is equitable to all students and to the intent of the original assessment. The main concern is that the students are given clear, timely, and explicit direction for the alternate assessment. Directions may require a short two to three minute video to support clarity and give students the opportunity for multiple viewings.

Students in special populations may require an alternate form of assessment. For example, this may require a music score being Brailed and physically mailed to a limited-sight student. Assessments with specific listening requirements may need to be altered to provide accessibility for students that are hearing impaired.

Students requiring alternate forms of assessment generally identify themselves for special considerations at the university level, however, students are asked to share the information specifically with their instructors. An inclusion about special considerations on a course syllabus can be a helpful reminder for all students.

Conclusion

We cannot predict the future and as such it remains challenging to decree all assessments to take place as planned. The 2020 Covid-19 pandemic highlighted many challenges encountered with online music assessments. Beyond the need to transition to remote music teaching overnight, assignments needed to transition into the online environment as well. The challenges resulting from isolation, social-distancing, and overall anxiety are notable as they have identified burnout in adults and college students (Arslan et al., 2020; Yildirim & Solmaz, 2020), negative effects on achieving the necessary level of flow in music performance (Habe et al., 2021), and the need to shift to alternate online music assessment (Schiavio et al., 2021). However, there are opportunities that can arise from alternate teaching approaches as evidenced in various studies on student learning in the pandemic (Alam, 2020) and specific studies exploring opportunities arising in online music teaching (Joseph & Lennox, 2021).

Questions for Personal Implementation

This chapter provides several examples for online music assessment. Think about your particular music discipline. What forms of online music assessment would be reasonable and authentic for your class?

Further questions to consider:

- To what extent are your online music assessments authentic?
- What is the instructor's role during and after online assessment?
- What technology should be used to support online music assessments?
- What criteria are used for assessment?

7

Assessment: Case Studies

Assessment plays a key role in learning; this is also supported in the data findings gathered from the case studies. The case studies further evidence the importance of how assessment can be scaffolded in the online learning content to support strong student learning outcomes. Overall, the case studies suggest that students are motivated to complete assessments when they have forms of autonomy and student engagement connected to the assessment. This means that multiple discussion questions or multiple assignment options can be helpful for engaging student interest. Furthermore, the use of both individual and group assessments can further support student community in the online classroom.

While each case study does not surface the same findings on the particular themes of assessment, instructors across all cases were found to use multiple forms of technology in their online assessments. The use of wikis, papers, video presentations, discussions, and more was found to be helpful tools for creating assessment activities. Ensuring authenticity to the discipline of music was a foundational element for which technology was used and how it was used. The scope of the projects was scaffolded within the course content to support strong student attainment of learning goals.

One of the notable challenges in online assessment was the overall uncertainty of crafting robust online activities that demonstrated student musical knowledge in an equivalent manner to F2F teaching.

Case 1

Instructors and students taking part in the surveys, interviews, and focus groups were part of an undergraduate online Bachelor of Music programme. The seven instructors and five students surfaced key understandings and perceptions in online music assessments. It was noted that each of the components of communication, design, and assessment was not viewed as a separate entity of itself but rather part of an interwoven and complex larger whole. Instructors taught all music theory, musicology, applied pedagogy, and music electives in the online environment. One key feature of this case is the opportunity for students to participate in a hybrid, dual-mode delivery. This meant that students were able to choose to come to class for their music learning or attend through the online live conference stream. Students identified as committing to a single form of class attendance (i.e., either via on campus or online) with both on campus and online students taking in the class at the same time.

Assessment Design

Overall, instructors in case one found themselves teaching online as both new teachers and new to teaching online. Interested in technology, the instructors found themselves engaging in teaching through approaches that they had previously been taught or using the new online learning approaches that they gleaned from institutional workshops.

Assessment design was often considered through the vision of course design. Students were assessed through reflective writing, research papers, video presentations about content topics, and discussion questions.

Assessment design was also used to encourage the development of community connection between students. This development of student interaction was seen to be an important aspect of experiential learning. For example, one instructor described the use of a large class project wherein 'They have a specific portion of the Messiah, and they have to present live, like this to the whole class at a specific time.' Students listen to specific recordings and then submit reflective responses about the musical excerpts.

Instructor Self-Assessment

A common instructional strategy identified by all faculty participants was the inclusion of instructor self-assessment. For example, throughout the interviews, faculty participants identified various recollections of how they used self-assessment as a tool to aid in their own online teaching learning process. Instructors remarked on how they reflected on their previous training as musicians to see if their current teaching provided their students with the appropriate content for moving forward in music learning.

Student Choice

Four out of the seven faculty members identified the need for assessment design to accommodate student choice. This meant that students were given multiple options when completing a specific assignment. When students were given options in their assignments, instructors identified a form of student agency and autonomy in the student. This supports the use of providing students with multiple assessment options.

Technology in Assessment

There was a lack of consistent data to suggest that one particular online learning task was more or less effective than another. For example, one faculty member found WIKIs and discussion forums challenging to engage students to provide divergent and meaningful responses. Another faculty member remarked that he found discussions to be an effective way to develop community and engagement among the online students. Meanwhile, another instructor expressed that he was still trying to explore how to get his students involved in discussions. The discussion questions and activities themselves were not revealed. As such, it is difficult to ascertain the reasons for the difference of effective use.

One faculty member remarked that some aspects of course design required flexibility, and therefore had a flexible and open response to it. For example, he stated, 'We could do a discussion board on those, but because I give them the choice, the discussion board is a rough format because you really need everybody to address the same prompt in the discussion board.' This 'rough format' was found to be more of an open prompt question that permitted students to engage in the learning from a variety of viewpoints and musical backgrounds.

Authentic to Discipline

Six faculty members viewed online activities as enabling students to achieve meaningful music learning provided that the students regarded the online learning environment itself as 'authentic' for their learning. This meant that the students themselves needed to perceive the online environment as effective. The term 'authentic' was associated with being helpful for furthering understanding and application of music learning.

However, authenticity of online learning was also challenged by the perceptions of instructors themselves. For example, one instructor, viewed face-to-face activities as more rigorous than online learning activities. He suggested the two environments resulted in different learning outcomes. He stated, 'I try to keep the same general format of the course but many of their assignments differ in both their scope and their application.' Meanwhile, another instructor held a different viewpoint. 'I don't make a distinction between online and face-to-face,' she stated. 'I think of them quite equally.' She noted that both forms of teaching could be equal in terms of providing students with well-rounded music learning outcomes. Together, these two statements evidenced that faculty members can hold different pedagogical perceptions of the face-to-face and online environments yet still facilitate learning in the online environment regarding the support for authenticity in teaching.

The seven faculty members expressed that applied music could be taught online yet suggested there were limitations which included latency issues. Hesitancy or possible challenges regarding online applied courses were identified as not only due to bandwidth issues for audio and video quality but required a necessary acumen for specialized music pedagogy for one's instrument or voice.

Individual and Group Assessment

The need for careful and considered pedagogical planning was described as a foundation for course design and overall content assessment. Faculty discussions evidenced the need for 'methodologies [to be] in place to allow synthesis to happen for students, as well as forethought for future pedagogical changes'. These perceptions on pedagogy also influenced the adoption of reflective assessments, such as planning for future semesters. One instructor described the need to examine his pedagogical planning through the eyes of his students. Concerned with student engagement and motivation, he often asked himself, 'How does this look to somebody else who's taking the course?' From this point of view, it can be suggested that online music instructors need to carefully consider each assessment activity and its position within the semester, and overall degree.

One of the keys to effective group assessment was the development of some level of trust and student voice within the student groups. Given the hybrid, or dual mode delivery of case one, it is interesting to note that data from the

Assessment: Case Studies 111

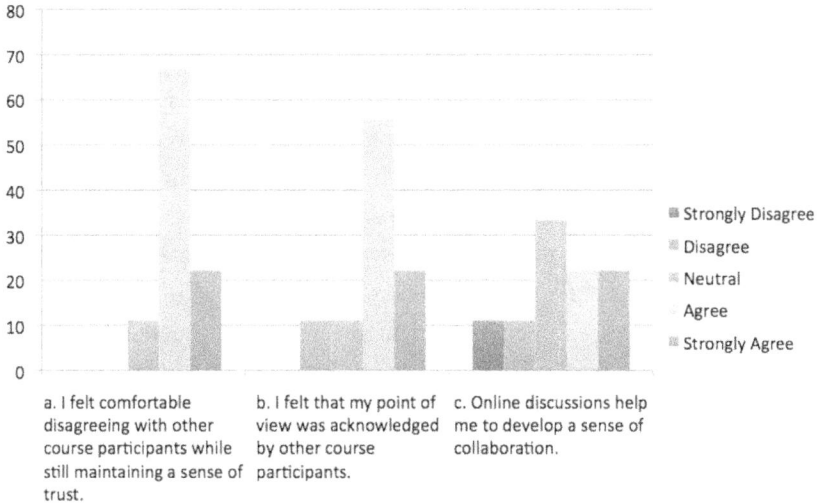

Figure 9 Comparison of Students' Perceptions Regarding Online Course Cohesion.

student surveys (n = 9) evidenced that students felt comfortable interacting within their class. While a number of students *Agreed* for students maintaining a feeling of trust during disagreement (88.9 per cent) and for students to feel their point of view acknowledged by other course participants (77.8 per cent), there was a mixture of perception about how online discussions develop a sense of collaboration among students (see Figure 9).

The topic of cheating was raised by both instructors and students during interviews. Cheating was suggested as something that could easily happen in online aural skills quizzes. One online student stated, 'If you wanted to, you can cheat. Sit by a piano and try to play it, too.' However, this same student acknowledged that cheating was not a viable option since dictation skills are needed for her future music performance. She acknowledged that because she wanted to become a performer, cheating was not an option for her.

Feedback in Assessment

One of the identified limitations within this case was the noted minimal use of peer feedback. One instructor remarked that students did not have the skills or knowledge base to provide constructive comments to other students due to the practical nature of the course. Another instructor saw the discussion forum as a one-way response activity rather than a dialogue between students. Overall, students were not encouraged nor were required to take up any form of peer review or peer feedback in the process of learning assessments. While these approaches are not supported in the research literature, the evidence of instructor mindsets prompts the need for further exploration in developing activities to engage students in peer-to-peer feedback.

Feedback in assessments was often described as providing grades, or marks. Specific descriptions of written or video commentary were not highlighted across the interviews. Through the student interviews, it was noted that students received automatic feedback from the use of online quizzes in classes. One student described the challenge of assessment feedback when she explained, 'It is helpful having quizzes and things online as long as the teacher goes back and reviews it.' Students also mentioned the inclusion of interactive technology that provided students with the ability to learn the content at any time and at their own pace.

Case 2

Case 2 portrays an online music education instructor, David, in a Bachelor of Music programme. He is very comfortable with technology and spent many years gaining skills in using technology to support to his students and the online music classroom.

Assessment Design

While David did incorporate learning tasks that were 'fun or different and not just fill in the bubble test', he also provided students with opportunities to develop musical scholarship. A final term project at the end of the course was one way that students were able to weave together their overall course learning. David explained, 'So I want students to write at the end. Just so there's something scholarly at the end and so that they can kind of articulate what they've learned, somehow.'

A diverse approach to assessment design was identified in this case. Assessments included group and individual projects, listening exams, creativity criterion, music culture exploration, and ensuring assessment allowed for kinaesthetic, audio, and video approaches. The learning tasks involved students and ensured that students had opportunities to demonstrate their understanding and creativity.

Authentic to Discipline

One of the key aspects of assessments for the instructor in case 2 was the purposeful and careful assessment design to ensure the assessment itself was both relatable and mirrored in the discipline of music. Going beyond research papers, the instructor found himself creating both individual and group assessment activities to ensure students had music knowledge as an individual to share with and among group members, as is common in a band ensemble. Supporting students through meeting the university librarian, sustained development for community communication and collaboration, and learning tasks that allowed students to experience virtual music instrument exploration through a virtual environment (e.g., Second Life) to teach the role of melody harmony and rhythm were just some of the assessment approaches the instructor threaded through his assessment design.

Students were given multiple ways to complete tasks and to ensure that they were able to show their content understanding. This meant that the learning tasks were built to consider individual, group, audio, visual, and hands-on learning opportunities. Group tasks allowed all learners to take up a specific portion of the activity and then come together to share their knowledge. Kinaesthetic assessment tasks included a virtual band tour as well as music projects that contextualize and set students up for awareness of future music careers. Overall, the learning tasks within a course were connected to each other and supported the learning objectives of the course.

Rubrics were part of a transparent and explicit knowledge support system for students. Exemplar models as well as inspirational and reward mechanisms were built into each course assessment.

Feedback in Assessment

Feedback was a deeply ingrained aspect of assessment. A focus on immediacy of feedback was apparent through the instructors use of SMS texting as well as the sharing of exemplary student work within the course. The immediacy of providing feedback to students on assessments was noted to relieve student anxiety among a busy semester.

Case 3

Case 3 highlights findings from a case study of five instructors that found themselves teaching music online without much experience in online music learning, but with extensive teaching and music education experiences.

Assessment Design

There were two approaches to course design that affected assessments: the approach to asynchronous course design and student expectations of course design. For example, two of the online courses represented in the study were similar to a correspondence course. These courses did not require regular, active participation with other students outside of posting a response to a discussion forum. Students in the online music courses expected their own understanding of flexibility, minimal building of community, and minimal course interaction.

Instructor Cathy suggested that the inclusion of student choice assisted her students in increased participation such as the options she provides her students within the discussion area. Robert further suggested that active participation in learning is highly important. Robin further parsed this importance when she stated, 'It kind of helps them merge those two worlds, [of personal and learning content].' However, as faculty members iterated as found with traditional courses, too, 'Some of them respond … and some of them do not, but that's to be expected with anything.'

Supporting Academic Integrity

In addition to building student learning through the process of the learning tasks, the learning task also was found to uphold academic integrity through its design and personalization. Cathy suggested,

> If the requirement is long enough, they would have a difficult time commissioning someone else to do this for them weekly … but also, if it's personal enough, that they have to and are also motivated to provide their own answer because somehow it's related to their opinion, to their review of the material, to their own additional research that they go in and add to it, they're less likely to – potentially – they are less likely to cheat.

Discussion Activities

Discussions were common in both course design formats (i.e., faculty created and 'boxed' course design). 'These are just a way to ensure that they are engaging in the course materials. It's a way of ensuring they are present,' explained Cathy. An important aspect for supporting student learning was the way in which students were expected to participate in the discussion forums. Cathy used the discussion for students to demonstrate their content knowledge. Robin used the discussion forum to hold debates 'to liven things up a bit'. In general, the discussion forums were used for students to not just regurgitate content, but to 'bring to the discussion more examples or something we haven't talked about that week', Cathy stated.

Listening Activities

As stated by Tjana, 'Listening is the most challenging for them ... they know how to read a book and study it, but they don't know how to deal with something that they can't hold in their hands,' like music. Faculty further identified that these students needed to be taught *how* to listen for rests, syncopations, instrumentation, etc. Tjana summed up the typical student taking the online music course when she said, 'This was a course for non-majors ... they are not musicians, many of them, not at all.' this implies that assessment activities need to address, or be designed for, the student audience as collective.

Feedback in Assessment

Learning tasks were not created to occupy students with mere writing tasks, but to have them interact with their learning. Instructor Cathy described the incorporation of film assignments, blog activities, discussion topic options, and individual projects as ways for students to personalize learning in her course. She provided feedback to each student on their tasks so that they were able to expand their thoughts and ideas. In addition to the use of rubrics and written grade feedback on assignments, Cathy remarked, 'It takes about 6 hours to respond to one set of discussion board posts.'

There was a noted challenge by faculty to identify particular ways to motivate students to participate in tasks beyond their grades. Instructor Robin remarked that she used 'extra credit' for getting students to participate more. She explained,

They're only responding to me when I am throwing out an extra credit carrot …
If I'm posting related articles or check this out, or listen to this, it's related to
what you just read, or let's talk about this, it's kind of radio silence.

Questions to Consider

From the case studies it is apparent that the individual instructors had unique approaches to assessment in their classes. Keys to each assessment included how the assessment was integrated into the semester structure as well as the relation of authenticity to future music careers. From this perspective:

- What assessment practices resemble most like your own?
- What assessment practices are very different from your practices?
- What challenges do you perceive as inhibiting the development of your online assessment activities?
- If technology was not an issue, what might your assessments look like?

Part Two

Practical Application

8

Considerations for Teaching Music Online

Introduction

As we turn to the current higher education crisis caused by the coronavirus, universities are facing critical questions regarding sustainability and scalability as the situation continues to unfold. The challenge of teaching beyond classroom walls is even more acute for performing arts faculties, like music performance, whose staff may be ill-equipped for agile online learning implementation.

A key challenge exposing music's limitation for shifting to online learning is its traditionally focused face-to-face teacher–apprenticeship teaching models. Moving forward in a Covid-19 world will likely challenge the pedagogical approaches used by many face-to-face higher education music academics. Addressing a pedagogical change to ensure continued excellence in music teaching is complex and stratified.

Research into teaching music online is not a new exploration (Keast, 2009); however, it is still limited in study. Studies show that music can be taught online in ways that further student musical understanding (Keast, 2009) as well as performance skills (Kruse et al., 2013), teaching internships (Pike, 2017), and music appreciation (Eakes, 2009). However, the complexity of offering online music classes surrounds the nature of teaching an *artform* from the audio and visual limitations of headphones or speakers, and a 2D screen. The best scenarios have yet to perfectly address all of the intricacies of a teaching music online. We are left with ontological questions, such as How do you teach art through a technology-mediated environment? And, how can a teacher create presence online?

These ontological questions will likely continue to be debated in forms for years to come. However, the critical matter for the future of music education involves supporting those who are teaching music online with the knowledge and skills in online design, assessment, and communication.

A 'lift and shift' of face-to-face (F2F) teaching methods to an LMS is discouraged. Teaching music online is different than its F2F counterpart (Johnson, 2017). It involves understanding the most effective components for teaching music in an online environment and having a teaching philosophy that supports the adoption (Johnson). From a leadership perspective, it requires acknowledgement of the importance of online learning for the sustainability and scalability of music education, and a change in how music programmes embed online classes (Johnson, 2018a).

Short-, medium-, and long-range planning will need to involve strategic forecasting and outlines for professional development programmes to support instructors in how they can effectively teach online. Students will also need helpful orientation to support their new learning platforms. While Covid-19 demanded a rapid online response, we now have opportunity to re-adjust and design for purposeful online music pedagogy by exploring, and evaluating, our own music teaching philosophy.

Teaching Philosophy

Now that we have explored the three main components of the framework, it is important that we address the central importance of teaching philosophy. In simple terms, our teaching philosophy is at the heart of why, and how, we teach. The decisions we make as instructors are influenced by what we believe and value. The complexity of how we interact with those beliefs and values on our teaching world creates our unique approach to teaching. From the use of a large teaching framework down to our concrete lesson plans, both the simple and complex teaching decisions come out of our beliefs and values of teaching. One would be remiss to not address this core influence on any framework or model in teaching.

When we consider our unique teaching philosophy for music, we should also take time to think about how we take up the following items that greatly impact our current teaching philosophy: Beliefs and Values, Self-Reflection in Teaching, Timing and Design, and Authenticity in Teaching. Together they influence our beliefs in the practice of teaching, and therefore will manifest as influences in how we choose to teach music online. Each of these items was shown, in some form, to influence how instructors approached teaching music online in the case studies. The core findings that surfaced the need for social constructivism in teaching music online and the connection to these topics are specifically addressed in the 'London Review of Education's Special Edition of Music Education' (Johnson, 2017). The paper explores the importance of having a social constructivist approach when teaching music online. Taking time to explore once beliefs and values and overall teaching philosophy is paramount when navigating the process for teaching music online.

To situate the importance of these influences with regard to teaching music online, and to signify the degree to which our teaching philosophy impacts our actions and interpretation of our world, teaching philosophy has been positioned at the core of the framework (see Figure 10). To this end, the following chapter explores five key areas to consider within your teaching philosophy. Understanding our individual beliefs and values and how they manifest in our current teaching will provide a helpful foundation for exploring the three components that make up the framework for teaching music online.

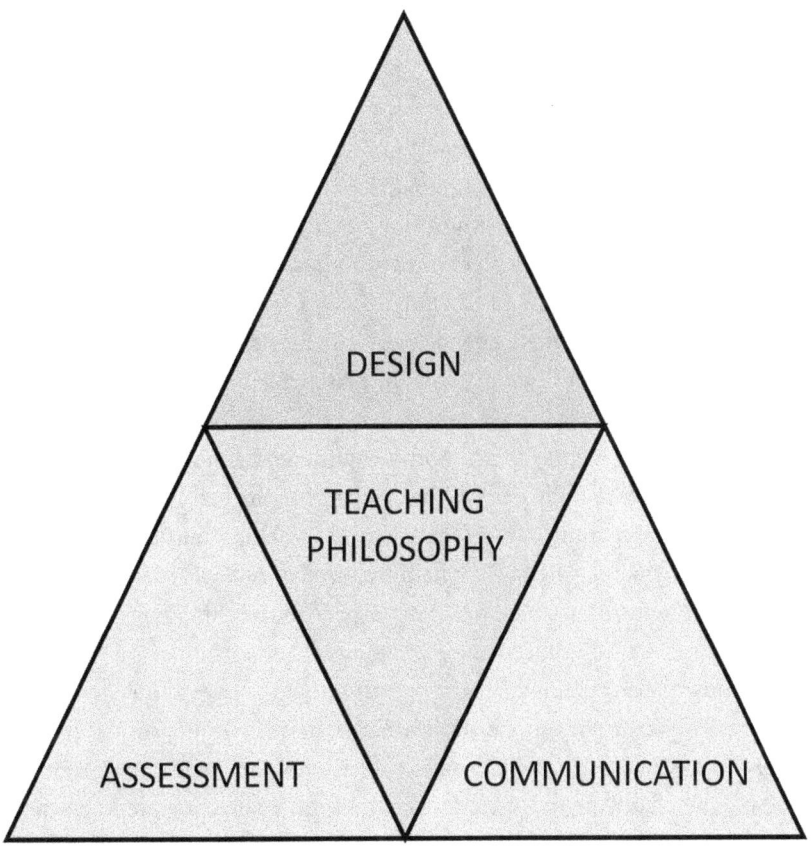

Figure 10 Basic Framework for Teaching Music Online.

Beliefs and Values

Beliefs and values present themselves in our teaching in all disciplines. Perhaps we value that a music teacher should be an expert musician before they can be a music teacher. Perhaps we value that our students are given experiences that support the integration of technologies such as apps, mobile devices, and digital instruments.

Each teaching activity we construct and lesson plan we create is built upon what we value and believe about teaching approaches. Teaching without exhibiting some form of our values and beliefs on teaching is difficult to say the least – not impossible, but very challenging. Our beliefs about teaching music online – whether it is a valid approach or not – will be somewhat evident to our students and colleagues. Perhaps it may not be an overt exclamation, but it becomes realized through the types of activities we use, time given to the creation of online content, the approach to design and many other components for teaching. Our values and beliefs can be key mechanisms for transforming of approach to teaching music online.

It can be suggested that there are many reasons for teaching music online. Some teachers come to teaching music online as a considered choice, whereas others come because they are 'voluntold'. It is important to know our 'why' as we begin to transform our teaching for the online environment. Knowing our purpose allows one to be better positioned to address possible bias and limitations that may become present in our teaching. For example, many higher education music teachers had to immediately deliver their music teaching through online delivery as a response to Covid-19 back in March 2020. This scenario provided opportunity for many to reconsider the use of technology in teaching online (e.g., teaching online was a stopgap until on-campus could resume, teaching online was an opportunity to both address the challenge of the pandemic and advance one's teaching skills in the use of technology for teaching music). Our purpose for teaching in general, whether implicitly realized or not, will eventually surface in some form or fashion. Therefore, our purpose for teaching music online, the 'WHY', will surface as well.

Both music and teaching have the opportunity to engage audiences through creativity. This creativity in music is what perhaps may appear as a certain feeling when we hear a particular note choice, lyric, or chord progression. For example, when listening to a melody, a composer may use a common harmonic progression and follow it up with a similar progression that ends, or moves through, an unexpected chord. Composers often use musical devices as ways to engage the listener, evoke a particular emotion, and even sometimes may use musical devices that allow for multiple interpretations. We can consider music teaching to use similar techniques. We use creativity to help make learning 'sticky'. It's that stickiness of learning that not only supports engagement of learning, but from a neuroscience perspective, we use bits of information we already have to activate new pathways in the brain to support memory retrieval, give students those 'ah-ha' learning moments, as well as support learner motivation.

Now let's not suggest that the complex harmonic structures used by composers are, or are not, equal in creative innovation to teaching a lesson on how to play a major scale. Both can be innovative in their own ways. Perhaps we would like to challenge ourselves to look at teaching as the opportunity to engage students in creative ways to better support personalization of learning for our music students. Teaching music online can be a creative teaching response to supporting this personalization.

It is from this perspective that I have embraced the online environment to teach music. It is about the opportunities for personalization of music learning. Just as a composer explores additional chord tones (such as the use of an unexpected minor IV chord in between a typical ii-V progression), the online environment, when carefully and purposefully structured, can provide a music student with a different experience for learning music. A different learning experience makes it personal to the student. This doesn't mean that everyone will like learning in the online environment, nor will every student flourish in that environment. But I would also suggest that our tastes in, and interpretation of music can also be viewed as unique to an individual.

Online environments and composition styles, or any other musical device, are not whimsical connections. On the contrary, it is the idea that we use tools or devices to support the development of music creativity. However, to achieve an innovative result in either one requires the use of foundational elements that need to be addressed when we consider teaching music – whether it be face-to-face teaching, online teaching, or any of its derivations in between. These foundational elements are the basis of our teaching pedagogy, whether we have a self-awareness of their use or not.

When we encounter an idea about music teaching, we make a choice as to whether or not we will use it in our future teaching. The ideas and pedagogical tools that we value come together to create our unique teaching pedagogy. Perhaps equally important questions to further ask yourself include: How can I explore these types of philosophical questions to help me understand what I perceive as important and effective for teaching music?

To get to the core of why we teach music online, we likely need to explore why we teach music in general. Is our purpose to inspire future musicians? Is it to maintain relevance to contemporary teaching and culture? There may not be a single answer to such a question, but it is a question that needs to be plumbed in our journey of teaching music online. This journey is like life – filled with opportunities to learn from our mistakes and to learn from others. Over these next few pages, continue to consider your WHY, and begin to explore how teaching music online may open doors not only for you to learn new approaches to teaching music, but to provide your students with opportunities to connect with music in ways that further personalize their learning and support them in achieving their music goals.

Self-Reflection in Teaching

The tools we use to teach may change over the course of our teaching career. This is a natural journey as we reflect on the teaching tools we use and how they have or have not supported our students' learning. Self-reflection is a key teaching tool found in a pedagogical toolbox.

Self-reflection is a regular experience for musicians as we reflect while we perform. The action of reflection involves active listening – that is, we listen and simultaneously make meaning while we listen. It is 'active' because we go beyond hearing or perceiving sounds. Active listening in music demands that detailed musical complexities are considered and contextualized for musical meaning (Mamlok, 2017) from that experience. Our music meaning is often considered against our previous knowledge and, if needed, a specific course of musical action is determined. All of this happens simultaneously while the musician is playing. We can experience this in our music teaching as well.

Reflection-in-Action

Termed by Schön (1983) as *reflection-in-action*, the process of reflective action is acted upon by both music performers and teachers, as an approach to in situ problem-solving. For example, when music-making, it may be a fleeting thought that creates a response to adjust a tempo or change a finger position. The posture of active listening helps us to know what is working well and what has opportunity for improvement.

In-the-moment reflection is also taken up by teachers to support the need for differentiated learning (Tomlinson, 2014). For example, a student's performance may prompt a music teacher to simultaneously reflect on what would be the most effective verbal feedback or moment-specific teachings during a music lesson. While we may not be consciously aware of all of pivots made during our teaching time, these adjustments can be creative acts akin to the act of creativity, or flow, as described by Csikszentmihalyi (1988) about music making.

Reflecting-on-Action

In addition to reflecting-in a teaching experience, we can reflect after an experience. The act of reflecting-on a completed action, or period of time, provides teachers with opportunity to consider broader learning contexts and applications for innovative teaching. This form of reflection can support the embracing of, and development of, new approaches to teaching. Schön (1983) stated that in this state of reflection, 'we reflect-on-action, thinking back on what we have done in order to discover how our knowing-in-action may have contributed to an unexpected outcome' (p. 26). More than a spontaneous response, reflection-on-action can provide the teacher to consider long-term reconceptualization that embrace alternative forms of teaching practices or strategies.

In teaching music online, reflection-on-action is a key pedagogical tool. When beginning to teach music online, one may reflect-on successful face-to-face teaching and activities to consider how they can be effectively transformed to the online environment. Given the pedagogical paradigm shift required when moving to online teaching, reflecting may include both considering how something was taught in the face-to-face environment and including using the online teaching scenario to innovate the learning experience.

Let's quickly compare the differences between these two tools. When teaching a music lesson online, you may have found yourself moving your camera to show your keyboard and then moving it back to a headshot position when you were speaking. Determining when and how to change camera angles or positions was reflection-in-action. After an online music lesson, we may find ourselves thinking back to the challenges of moving around a single camera and consider alternatives, such as having two cameras. This is an example of reflection-on-action. While simplistic in idea, these two reflective tools are integral to making any music class an effective learning environment for our students.

Teachers also engage in reflection when using backwards design (Wiggins, Wiggins, & McTighe, 2005) to ensure that class content scaffolds in a cumulative manner such that students can successfully complete the semester recitals and assignments. The tool of self-reflection is not only used by teachers to develop effective scaffolding of class design and course content, but it is also used during those in-the-moment teaching scenarios.

As musicians, we listen to our performance and make necessary musical and functional modifications to fine tune the performance. In the online environment, and even more specifically when teaching online through video streaming, music teachers find themselves using the process of reflection-in-action as they may quickly navigate to YouTube for a just-in-time musical sample or position their saxophone closer to the camera when demonstrating a finger movement. Verbal dialogue is conveyed to seek confirmation of usefulness of the example. Online teachers navigate through this reflective process during the video stream, as well as after the stream has closed. This is helpful while the task is happening, as well as after the task has finished.

Timing and Design

Sometimes tools are used together – and this is an example of such a case. Because of the nature of the online environment, as we explore when activities happen in the online environment, we also need to consider how activities are designed for meaningful engagement. This means that when we decide the timing of an activity (i.e., asynchronous or synchronous), there are specific design considerations that will be taken up. Let's take a moment to consider how these tools work together.

When we think of timing as a tool, it is generally in regard to a boundary of time. That is, time as bounded by hours on a clock. However, in online learning, we use time to frame the way an activity is experienced: we can learn together at the same moment in time and across different time zones (i.e., synchronously) or we can learn at different times of the day or week (i.e., asynchronously). Both approaches support a shared learning experience that aim to position students for exchanging ideas.

Asynchronous learning can support and extend learning activities in a variety of ways. For example, students can watch a video, contribute to an online reading group, complete a quiz or online activity, or add to a text, video or audio discussion at a time that is suitable for the student. Asynchronous timing provides students with flexibility of scheduling that can be used to support employment activities and various family life needs. These types of activities can be adapted or changed as needed. However, the activity itself needs to be carefully crafted and outlined before students can take part. Typically, this means that the design is more static in nature. The clarity of design also support ease in the direction of the task and steps for completion.

It is noted that asynchronous learning can support more complex activities and tasks. For example, a student group could be tasked with facilitating an online task. Again, this calls for an intricate and detailed attention to design.

Synchronous learning also supports student learning through meaningful engagement across distances, yet it occurs in real time. The use of synchronous activities promotes an immediacy of collaboration. For example, pair and share activities, video conference group discussions, and practice sessions provide students with opportunity for immediate feedback. Whether it be feedback from peers or instructor, there is opportunity for dynamic flow with discussion activities, live recital performances, real-time practice sessions, and in-class individual or group presentations. Clarity of design is for some, easier to adjust in the synchronous environment due to the real-time nature of the learning and ability to provide in-the-moment explanations and directions. The challenges of synchronous activities in the online environment are generally in the areas of technology use and the access to consistent internet bandwidth.

The tools of timing and design clarity are intricately woven into online learning. Johnson's (2020) conceptual model for online music learning begins to unpack general considerations for teaching music with technology. It suggests that there is a method of discovery through examining teaching approaches, ways of learning and the timing of the online technology environment before one can focus on the central aspects of learning – i.e., student skills and knowledge.

The inner function of the model – operationalizing effective student learning – is the proverbial holy grail of teaching music online. As researchers we are intrigued and drawn to examine the extent to which music content and assessment can effectively be taught using the online environment.

Authenticity in Teaching

One of the challenges often raised when discussing teaching music online is the question: to what extent can music, or any art form, be embodied, and therefore taught, across an online platform? While there are many responses, assumptions and ontological thoughts that need to be carefully examined as individuals respond to that question, perhaps there can be some insights through the considered lens of authenticity in teaching.

Authenticity can be addressed in different ways but the focus here is on authenticity to the discipline. In simple terms, this means what we teach is tied to the real-world nature of the discipline. Framed within online music teaching, it means that how and what we teach is linked to the career of a musician and taught in the online environment.

The online environment can support our students with learning activities that we are not able to action or take up in the face-to-face classroom (Bourne et al., 2005). In terms of teaching music online, the online environment can provide our students with musicians located across the world. Where it was once financially and time-limiting to have students meet, connect, and ask questions with a world-renowned performer, the online environment opens the doorway for students to have asynchronous and synchronous masterclasses, workshops, and discussions.

But as we add in these additional forms of learning activities, it is important that we use our tool of authenticity to gauge the relevance of the activity for our music students.

Kim Koh (2017) in her research on authentic assessment examined seminal literature to elucidate criteria that can help guide in the creation and evaluation of authentic assessment. Given the importance of assessment to teaching, that is, 'the process is as important as the product' (p. 3), there are critical links throughout the teaching design process that require authenticity to the discipline be manifested in the teaching process. These design keys include: the use of open-ended tasks for real-world problems; engagement in 'complex and ill-structured problems' (p. 5); development of 'positive habits of mind, growth mindset, resilience, and grit, and self-directed learning' (p. 5). When viewed from this perspective, the pedagogical tool of authenticity becomes a tool that enables music students to tackle musical challenges of today to become musicians positioned for a career in music tomorrow.

The pedagogical tool of authenticity is our encompassing lens for teaching music online. Instead of asking ourselves whether to use a particular technology tool or online activity, our question becomes, how does this learning experience relate to a career in music? For example, while we may not need students to record their ensemble parts in a face-to-face classroom, in an online music classroom, we can evaluate such a learning activity as authentic to a music career, as well as an avenue for supporting personalized learning.

Institutional Parameters

Stability and visionary fortitude are qualities that enable educational institutions to persist in sustainability, scalability, and accessibility. As a result:

> Educational institutions tend to apply traditional classroom ideas and pedagogy in non-contiguous collaborative learning environments, assuming that since these environments allow the interaction that we see in the classroom (e.g., chat, real-time meetings, and shared applications) traditional pedagogy can be used. Unfortunately, these environments do not support such interactions in the same way that it occurs in face-to-face (time delay, lack of complete sensory contact, non-availability of off task activities, etc.).
>
> (Kirschner et al., 2004, p. 47)

Single ideas by themselves have finite endpoints. Ideas created in collaboration can, together, amass insurmountable heights. Currently, educational leaders are faced with how to best incorporate e-learning into organizations that were historically built upon the tangible – buildings, books, and face-to-face lectures.

Through this process of change, both educational administration and faculty are charged with becoming exemplars of great learners to solve the impending issues at hand.

It will take a collaborative effort of ideas and actions as we seek to resolve the questions of technology implementation. This means, 'sustained changed in behaviour is unlikely unless it is accompanied by deeper changes in teachers' attitudes and beliefs (and unless the context in which teachers work is supportive of the change being promoted)' (Borg, 2018, p. 202). Engaging in deliberate collaborative communities will enable a mirroring of the necessary teaching paradigm shift: collaboration in the classrooms, research faculty, and administrative offices. This juncture requires action by all stakeholders. Since meaningful learning is not a transfer or ideas, but a *transformation* of understanding, the transformation necessitates action from all involved parties. This collaborative community, specifically faculty and administration, will need to actively address modifications towards the scholarship of teaching and learning and the embracing of collegial equity in research, teaching, and learning.

The central question of this technological shift: 'How are students given opportunity to engage in transformational learning throughout their academic career?'

Theoretically possible, this question involves effective and efficient practicality. It is to this end that student learning must involve active participation. Identified decades earlier, this type of active learning was termed constructivism by Vygotsky (1978). A meaningful learning experience for music students suggests the integration of multiple learning components involving reading music, writing music, listening to music, playing music, and teaching music.

Further research by Bandura (1981) described learning as more than an individual event, but a social experience (i.e., social constructivism). This implies collaboration. Together, the impact of learning, as both individual and social events, heightens persistence, motivation, and intrinsic and external rewards for strong student engagement. Identified in online learning research, without meaningful learning, students can fall prey to attrition (Picciano, 2002). The elements of leadership, faculty collaboration, and student engagement create the nexus of the institution known as formal education. Without all three elements involved, an institution will not function effectively, nor navigate the uncertainty of pending technological change (i.e., blended and online learning). How each figure addresses innovative technology for teaching and learning becomes critical. Fully dependent on each other, there is a necessary co-constructed response that will support, or impede, the future of music education.

Next Steps

Take time to outline and map your personal teaching philosophy and teaching influences.

Questions for Personal Implementation

Begin to reflect of aspects of your teaching approach that 'just happened' over time.

- What are ways that you can examine and re-adjust any aspects of your teaching philosophy that do not align to your beliefs and values?
- Secondly, how might you be influencing your institution, and your institution influencing you?

9

Designing Your Online Teaching Space

Online Music Course Design: A 20,000-Foot View

The practical aspect of course design contains three main steps: plan, create, and adjustment. These steps are often reiterated by instructors from the case studies and the instructional design literature. The following section briefly outlines key items for each step.

Plan

1. Plan to use a course design timeline. Take time to locate or create a timeline organizer. This organizer will be used to map out the topics, activities, and assessments that need to take place a cross the semester. Keep the layout brief and succinct.
2. Identify learning objectives and plan for instructional design. On a separate piece of paper, outline the learning objectives and specific topics that you need to cover for your course. Reorder and organize the topics so that each learning objective is met and the overall content knowledge constantly builds towards a final large topic goal.
3. Plan to incorporate backward design. Sometimes it is easier to start with the ultimate learning goal in mind, and then map the learning content backwards. For example, if the goal is to learn how to arrange for a small ensemble, backwards design would include the topics of creating duet arrangements, then trio arrangements then quartets, and so on.
4. Plan how to address prioritized learning concepts. There are many components that can be taught with regard to a specific topic. However, not every component may be necessary. Consider and address the prioritized and key learning concepts for each of your topics.

5. Plan appropriate video and text content learning and online learning interactions/activities. At this point, there should be topics outlined for each week in your organizer. Identify what content will be highlighted in each topic and the corresponding online activities or interactions that should take place. This includes identifying readings and videos with their time allocations.
6. Plan to appeal to student evaluation and learner diversity (e.g., full-time work). After you have your basic map of your semester, look at your timeline through the eyes of a student with a full-time job. Make adaptations to ensure that each week has an equal workload that is commensurate with the programme requirements.
7. Plan for course flexibility. Given the nature of technology, and the changing world at large, it is helpful to include small windows of time for adoption within this semester. Perhaps this means having a TBA short reading in week four and week eight. This allows for you to address specific learning and current topics arising from your students during the semester.
8. Plan to take time to plan. Include opportunities across your semester plan for you to make notes for redesign an adjustment of future additions of the class. Also, ensure to give yourself enough time to create and adjust your course design before the semester begins.

Create

1. Create text content. Using your completed timeline organizer, begin to create content for each topic in a separate document. Name each document according to the week and topic. Save the documents in a single folder titled 'online content'.
2. Create introductory and housekeeping content. Take time to create a short 2–3-minute video introduction of yourself. Include not only your interest in the course topic, but perhaps a bit of your own personal background and career in music. This is often the first impression students will have of you as their online teacher. Create optional information pages, such as strategies for discussion posts, frequently asked questions, and helpful music resource links.
3. Create video content. For each topic, create a short three-to-four minute content video that highlights key items from the content. Include key questions students should be considering as they learn about the content.

It is often helpful to create video scripts prior to making a video. A script can be easily changed for a future re purposing.
4. Create weekly student organizer. At the top of each weekly topic document, outline the students' tasks and responsibilities. For example, this may include readings, viewings, and synchronous discussion. Be sure to include deadlines with dates and times.
5. Create assessments. For each assessment, ensure there are multiple ways for students to individualize their response. Ensure the assessment is authentic to your particular music discipline and supports active learning.
6. Create online course area. Using the text and video documents created above, begin to piece together each online module/folder. Use similar fonts and colours for heading levels.
7. Create and activate areas for participatory interaction. This includes the use of course cafes, weekly informal synchronous sessions, online chat tools, and 24/7 video conference tools.
8. Create a backup plan. Identify how you will correspond with students should technology glitch. For example, take time in your introductory video to let students know that if there is a connection disruption to asynchronous session, you will continue to try to join this session, or send an announcement to all students.

Adjustment

The adjustment phase is a natural part of course design and can be suggested as an iterative course design cycle. When faculty are open to a cyclical process there is often less anxiousness and concern as a regular adjustment cycle can ensure a well-designed online course.

1. Confirm reasonable student workload. Once you have finished creating the online class area, take time to recalculate the student workload required. Ensure that the class is both rigorous but reasonable in workload and time required.
2. In-course design evaluation. Explore your online course area four possible misalignment of information. For example: are all of the deadlines the same as outlined in the course syllabus? Are the assignment directions equivalent wherever noted in the online area? How many clicks does it take to get to the assessment page from the original course homepage? Aim to organize your online content area to minimize student confusion and questions.

3. Peer Review. Invite a peer instructor to go through your online course and highlight any aspects that may be unclear or not intuitive. Reciprocate this gesture to your fellow peers.

Key Online Resources (for Performance Classes and Non-performance Classes)

The challenge of creating and locating resources in an organized manner is another aspect of design organization (see Chapter 4). Resources take time to develop and may mean allocating specific time during the week, or month, for this kind of development. There are many different kinds of resources that support and extend student learning. Helpful resources to include in an online music class are outlined below. These are not a finite list, but a starting place to provide some ideas to ponder regarding the development of supportive online resources to extend music student learning.

Performance Classes

- Video performance resources
- Links to music stores and music websites
- Online instrument tuner or tuner app
- Notation applications (Muse score, Finale, Sibelius, Noteflight, etc.) as well as links to videos on how to use specific notation applications
- Sample video warmups, written scale exercises, or practice background tracks
- Recording apps (Soundtrap, Bandcamp, GarageBand) and links
- Instrument care and maintenance information
- Expectations and requirements of recorded technical and performance exams
- Explicit instructions on how to record and submit technical and performance exams
- Blank manuscript paper PDF
- Play along audio recordings as well as backing track recordings for student practice

Non-performance Classes

- Frequently asked questions (FAQ) page
- Individual weekly modules or topic-based modules which will also contain weekly PowerPoint slides, handouts, and any other pertinent resources for the week

- Weekly schedule that includes an overview of topics to be covered in the semester
- Assessment descriptions and expectations
- Academic integrity and plagiarism documents
- Expectations for participation in synchronous discussions and breakouts
- Syllabus or course guide available as downloadable PDF

The resource list is only a starting place. Perhaps it might be helpful to ask, *How are these items currently used in your online teaching*? If there are some items that you think would be helpful to implement in your online teaching, the creation of a year-long resource development outline might support a systematic approach to increasing your current online teaching resources. A planned approach means we can add in teaching resources from the list in a manageable way. Remember, it's one step at a time. For one instructor, it might mean creating one additional video resource a month – that amounts to twelve new video resources in a year. For another instructor, it may result in starting an online organizer (e.g., Diigo.com) that allows for the instructor to add to the organizer whenever an appropriate new web resource is found.

Choosing between Asynchronous or Synchronous Online Music Teaching

The following section outlines the various steps and decisions that need to be made when developing an online music class. It is most helpful to explore the decisions in the order specified, as the outcomes of each decision can influence later opportunities. One of the first decisions that need to be made when developing an online music course is the question: 'Is the class to be asynchronous or synchronous?'

Asynchronous Online Music Courses Considerations

Asynchronous classes, no matter if they are academic or music performance focused, provide students with flexibility to complete the course contents on their own time across the semester. Normally students will begin and asynchronous timed course at the start of a semester as per other face-to-face classes. One of the decisions that need to be made by the instructor is *to what extent is the course asynchronous*?

There are two types of asynchronous courses: asynchronous across the weekly modules, and asynchronous across the entire term. Asynchronous format across weekly modules provides a student with flexible opportunity to complete the tasks anytime during a seven-day week period. Students stay within a bounded weekly schedule to accomplish course tasks and learning outcomes. Asynchronous classes across a semester are intricately designed such that the students are lock-stepped through LMS restricted releases according to completion of activities. Both formats have opportunities and challenges and are generally determined by school learning culture.

One of the challenges with a fully asynchronous class across this semester can be when students choose to complete a semester of work in a less than ideal length of time period. For example, as noted in Case Study 3, students erroneously expected to complete their music history course in a week's time. Misunderstood expectations can create challenges from an instructor point of view – due to multiple assessments of projects happening at non-scheduled times across the semester – and also challenges for students who do not allow enough time to reasonably take up and learn the new knowledge for the benefit of long-term memory.

When developing an asynchronous course, helpful student tools include resources for technology use, detailed checklists for weekly studies, opportunities for students to have formal or informal asynchronous discussions at specific times each week, as well as ensuring learning content is lock-stepped with instructional design released content.

With asynchronous activities that require students to contribute or collaborate with other students, such as asynchronous group projects, it is often helpful to provide students with specific weekly, or monthly, deadlines. In the case of online discussions, breaking the activity into two posts – initial post and reply post – ensures clarity of direction as well as activity function. For example, requiring students to submit their initial post by Thursday and a reply post by Sunday supports students who may have carer and work responsibilities during the week, as well as those students that are wanting to complete schoolwork on the weekend.

Synchronous Online Music Course Considerations

Synchronous music courses are often developed similarly in topic and weekly design akin to their face-to-face equivalent. The main difference is that the synchronous, or live, portion of the class occurs in a live video conference stream. When using this auction, ensuring students feel community within the class as well as quote presents quote from the instructor becomes key to sustaining interest and motivation across the semester. This aspect of the course can be considered similar to those face-to-face classes wherein students come to class because they feel there is a connection made and deeper meaningful learning happening when in the room.

Dual-Mode Teaching

Since the start of the 2020 pandemic, the opportunity and functionality for dual-mode teaching have come to the forefront. Dual-mode teaching means that the instructor is teaching from the classroom, with students in the classroom and online. The advantage of this mode of teaching is that students both near and far can complete their classes. Challenges with this mode of teaching include: a fully equipped technology classroom, carefully developed lesson plans for each class, development of equitable activities for those students in the classroom, and those students online, developing student community across both, an instructor with advanced technology skills who can troubleshoot technology issues on the fly.

One of the key considerations before choosing dual-mode teaching is the consideration of instructor aptitude for dual-mode teaching. This form of teaching requires heavy cognitive load due to the nature of interacting with students simultaneously in class, and online (see set-up recommendations below).

It is acknowledged that teacher preference and teacher technology skills can support or hinder dual-mode music teaching. This form of teaching may not be an option for all. It is recommended that teachers have an opportunity to try this form of teaching for the duration of a class prior to committing to a semester of dual-mode teaching.

Set-Up Recommendations

Asynchronous Course Set-Up

The set-up for teaching asynchronous online music classes requires the front load design of learning content. This means that content for each module, or weekly module, needs to be planned, designed, and content artefacts created *before* the course itself becomes activated for students. The recommended time to allocate for the creation of a twelve-week course is approximately six months. This allows for the full development of the syllabus with learning objectives, weekly learning contents artefacts (e.g., text, graphics, and video content), plus the creation of interactive learning tasks. The importance of students interacting with their learning cannot be undervalued. Even having students create short, three-minute videos providing their commentary or thoughts about the weekly content can be helpful in promoting so for flexion and metacognitive learning.

Synchronous Course Set-Up

Synchronous online music teaching generally mirrors a face-to-face class except those students do not attend a classroom. Instead, during that pre-scheduled weekly class time, students join the class through a live video conference stream. Pre-organization of classes is completed in a similar format to face-to-face class organization adhering to learning objectives, and overall assessments. Often, the online LMS area is used to provide students with a weekly archive of class materials, as well as technology tools to use to further support community discussion among students, and providing students with further links, videos, and access to readings. It is common for an instructor to share lecture slides, or PDF, twenty-four hours in advance of the class as a student support.

LMS organization often follows a similar structure of weekly modules to support intuitive and clear online class design. Supportive technology tools, such as calendaring of due dates, inclusion of weekly checklists, and class announcements, are commonly used.

Dual-Mode Teaching

Purposeful design of the dual-mode class requires time and an involved classroom and technology set-up. Essentially, the teacher is ensuring students in the classroom can see and hear all necessary content, while students in the online classroom are not restricted by classroom movement of the instructor. A helpful classroom set-up involves the use of two computers, an additional large monitor, an overhead projector, an external microphone, an external webcam, and various cables.

Having two computers running simultaneously permits two specific instructor instances in the video conference stream. This means one computer can provide a camera angle aimed at the front of the class, while the second camera instance can provide an alternate angle in the classroom. The important use of two cameras cannot be underscored. The multiple views allow students online to feel any small nuances in class that helps support community as well as musical gestures. *IF* you are an instructor that moves around the classroom a lot, consider placing tape on the floor as a reminder of the best place to stand for the online students to see you through the cameras. The addition of the second computer allows for the instructor to show and supply lecture slides to the classroom as well as live-streamed to the online students.

To help support ease of instruction for the instructor, it is helpful to place an external monitor on a chair next to an in-class student to support the acknowledgement and communication exchange with online students during the class. This monitor would be large enough for the teacher to see all online students faces in the online video conference software. For example, with the instructor at the front of the classroom, and screen behind them, students in class can be seated on chairs from both the centre and right side of the room. Placing the external monitor on the left side of the room each class allows for predictability for the instructor to engage with both online and on campus students consistently and equitably.

The use of the overhead projector is for both teaching and creating community. Similar to the face-to-face class, images of the instructor's lecture slides are presented on the screen at the front of the class. In addition, the video stream with online student video instances should also appear on the screen. This means that the instructor needs to space both applications appropriately on screen. It can be useful to have online student video instances on the same side of the screen during every class.

External microphone placement should be close to both the instructor and in-class students. The quality of external microphone should not be understated. An omni-directional, small cardioid microphone with USB connection is favourable. While there can be additions of audio input and monitor boxes with XLR microphones on mic stands, this can over complicate dual-mode delivery class set-up.

Two webcams are found to be supportive for instruction clarity and developing presence. Positioning a webcam on the external monitor ensures that when the instructor looks at the online students, those students perceive the instructor looking at them on their screen at home. This can be a key to ensuring instructor to student connection. Also, this set-up provides simplicity and decreased cognitive load. The second camera should be set up such that the online students can see students in class. Given that in-class students are shown the video conference stream of online students next to the lecture slides,

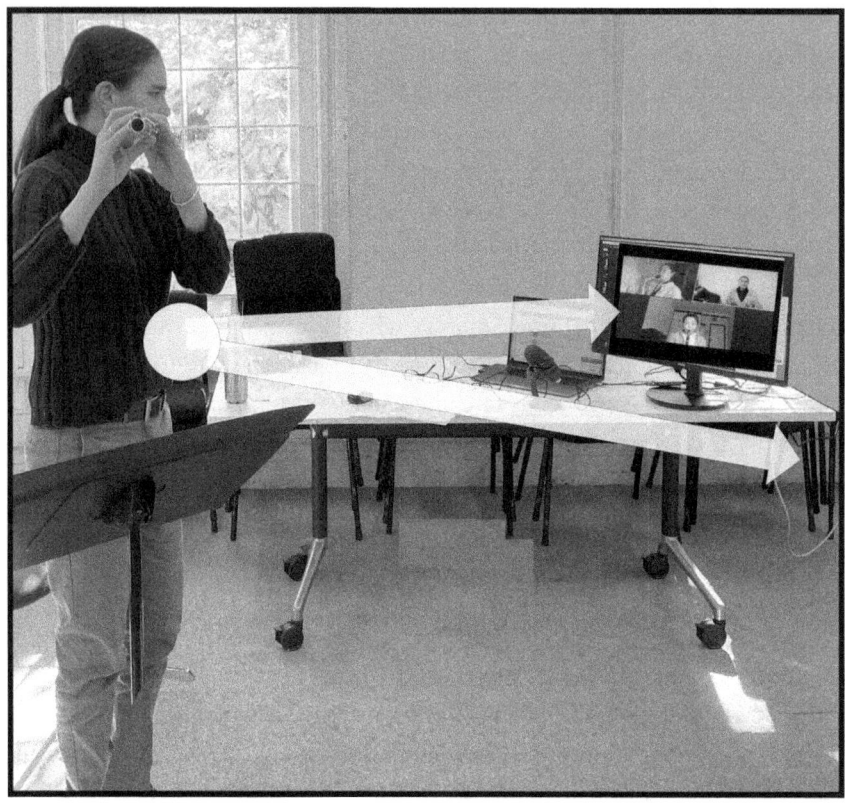

Figure 11 Dual-Mode Teaching Set-Up.

equity of community suggests online students have a similar visual of their on campus classmates.

There can be many cables, peripherals, and additional hardware and software incorporated into the dual-mode class. Recommendations include using an Ethernet-connected internet for stability of video conference transmission, 10 feet of HDMI cable, multiple extension cords and power strips, music stands, and one or two long tables. See Figure 11.

Activities in the dual-mode teaching environment include the use of simultaneous activities between online and in-class students, as well as separated activities for each student grouping. One supportive learning activity can be the use of playing together. Because of latency, having all students performed together, and hear each other, may not be an option. Therefore, creating opportunities for students to experience different learning tasks during a performance activity may be helpful for on-campus activities.

Practical Synchronous Session Backup Plans

Technology challenges and glitches can and will happen. The following six suggestions can provide students with expectations for resolving or problematizing technology issues.

- Turn off video if there is low internet bandwidth or reliability
- Have a text student identified as a support for class
- Create an expectation that students will re-join the video should their internet connection drop out
- Ask students to email or communicate with instructor if their technology is unstable or not available for live sessions
- Create a short 15–20-minute video on the synchronous content discussed and distribute via the LMS
- Create a video overview to highlight the key topics presented in each synchronous class and archive in the weekly LMS module area

Online LMS Area Organization and Design

The LMS area for both an asynchronous and synchronous music course should include the following basic items: welcome page, syllabus, instructor welcome and contact information, assessment information and directions for submission, separate weekly content folders, calendar with assignment due dates, and access two key institutional policies and learning supports. The offline design of the learning content should be organized in folders that mimic the online LMS area for easiest retrieval.

Some instructors may find it helpful to use the following graphic organizers (Figure 12 and Figure 13) to help identify elements for effective online course organization.

Once a folder system has been established on a computer desktop, it is easy to replicate the items as web pages or documents in the online course area. Figure 14 provides an example of the stepped structure of the online LMS folder organization.

Each online course area should release a weekly instructor video announcement. These should be created *during* the semester to allow for the video content to highlight current student comments as well as highlight specific weekly items and upcoming assignments and activities.

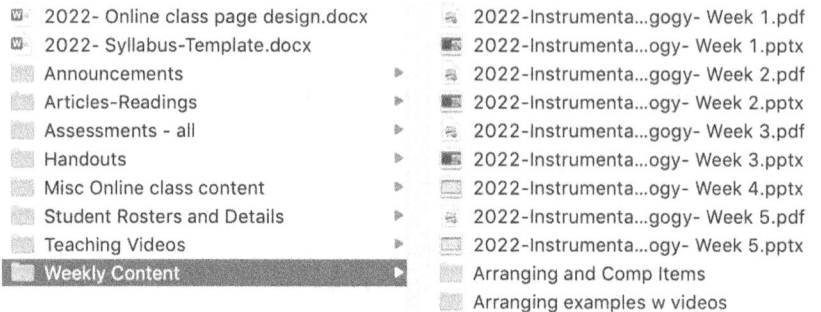

Figure 12 Weekly Content Folder Organization.

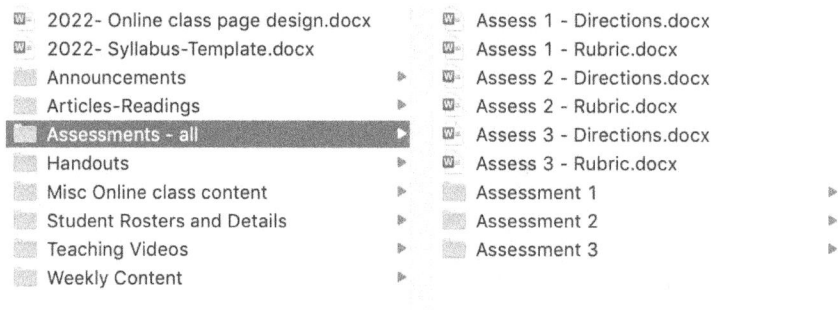

Figure 13 Assessment Folder Organization.

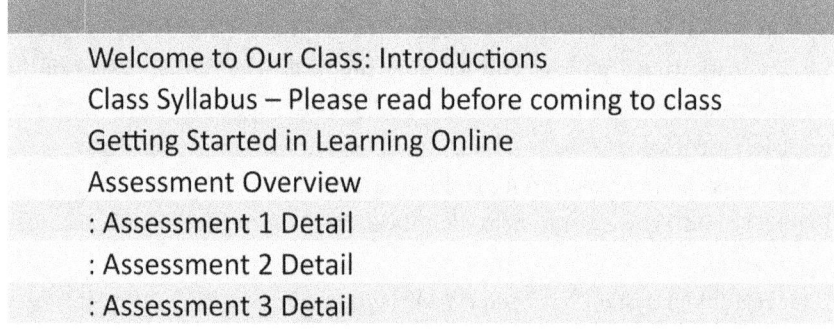

Figure 14 Stepped-LMS Document/Folder Organization.

It is noted that if the online music course is a weekly asynchronous format, course content should only reveal a maximum of three or four weeks in advance. Having the entire detail of the full semester's weekly modules revealed to students from day one can be overwhelming to the students. Further, some students may misunderstand the expectation of only completing one week at a time. This also provides the instructor with the opportunity to tweak upcoming weekly folders that may have yet to be revealed to students. Once a weekly folder has been made accessible to students, course content change is to be discouraged.

Re-Use and Re-Purpose

Another advantage of online learning is the ease of course and resource adaptation. Now this doesn't mean that instructors use the exact same materials in the exact same way each time the course is taught. Like the regular classroom, new research, and new ideas and thoughts need to be interspersed. However, the focused content of the course can be easily edited and updated. Long gone are the overhead pages with updates typed in. A new activity can be updated with the upload of your revised document. (Although, we need to remember that once the course content is revealed to the students, making changes to that content on the fly becomes very challenging.)

However, there are challenges with course adaptation – and the main one generally occurs due to cost-cutting efforts of administration when an instructor is asked to teach an online course they did not create or have some influence during its creation. While this repurposing can appear cost-effective (i.e., the instructor does not take time to update course content), various problems incur. Possible challenges include limited instructor knowledge of the online content, limited knowledge on the development of the assessments across the entire course structure, or even degree programme, and, last but not least, videos, or announcements that use the previous instructor's voice or appearance. While there can be valid reasons for an instructor redeployment, the person taking over a pre-created online course should take extra care to ensure that timed contents have been updated, and a familiarity has been attained.

Each of our online course areas should have some unique qualities of instructor personalization. Yes, there are similar elements like using a discussion forum, or uploading an assignment, but how students work towards these activities can be just as unique as your traditional class.

Creating Presence in Video Communications

A video can provide students with an opportunity to make a connection with the instructor. As outlined by Noetel and colleagues (2021), the hearing of auditory sounds and seeing specific graphics or visuals can support our neurological connection for understanding and overall improve student learning in higher education. This suggests that online LMS areas should provide students with video resources to further support and explain learning content.

For some, creating video for teaching can be a new experience. The following four items can be considered when creating video communications: clarity of message, opportunity for student inquiry, on screen focus, and speaker position on screen.

Clarity of Message

When creating video communications, the rule of thumb is to keep the video to a reasonable length of time such as five to seven minutes. Preparation of a basic script or talking points is often helpful to keep the video focused and targeted. Highlighting three or four key points and using graphics that directly illuminate the points are most effective. Taking time to practice reading the script can also ensure and ease of flow in the video.

Opportunity for Student Inquiry

Creating a video that allows for students to engage with the learning content can be as simple as having the speaker pause in the video and ask a question. Pausing after asking the question or directing the student to stop the video and respond on paper or in a discussion area is an opportunity for active learning. Video apps that allow for H5P are supportive tools that easily integrate student questions, quizzes, and interactive learning.

On-Screen Focus

When creating a video, it is important to consider the background behind the speaker as well as the speaker's appearance and overall surroundings. Non-distracting backgrounds such as a blank wall or non-cluttered bookcase can be helpful to maintain focus on the speaker. Furthermore, choosing colours and patterns that film well can also assist in supporting focus in videos.

Speaker Position on Screen

Lastly, how the speaker's image is framed in the video can help support overall connection between the viewer and the speaker. If we think about television newscasts, we often will see the speaker filmed from three positions: to the right to the left or to the centre of screen. This filming positioning supports the rule of thirds wherein the viewer's eye is directed to a particular part of the screen. When the speaker is to the left or to the right of the screen, there is a larger free space that supports a visual focus on the speaker. This camera technique, when combined with the speaker looking directly into the camera, helps to welcome and connect with the viewer. When the speaker looks beyond, or off camera, the viewer perceives a disconnect with the speaker. Finally, a close up of a speaker's facial image appearing across the entire screen should be used sparingly. This filming technique often suggests intense or authoritative demeanour. Taking time to experiment with different speaker positioning within the video screen can be a meaningful and helpful learning experience.

Copyright Compliance

It is important to consider copyright compliance when creating an online music course. While it is outside the scope of this book to address the varying policies on copyrights around the world, it is essential to highlight the need for each instructor to be acquainted with, and uphold, copyright. Music copyright, as well as publication copyright, video copyright, etc. have different complexities and fair use opportunities. Understanding and adhering to copyright is an essential part of teaching music online.

Achieving Successful Changes to Your Online Teaching

Creating a well-structured and meaningful online music course is not created overnight. As such, instructors may need to set specific monthly goals to help support meeting course creation deadlines. Identifying specific goals and priorities (e.g., create five learning objectives; create a new collaborative learning task) can be helpful task organizers. Furthermore, task organizers may need to be revised over time to ensure that they are obtainable, as well as realistic within a time frame. Modelling similar expectations required of students (i.e., calendaring goals, scheduling course creation time, etc.) are often helpful in achieving successful development and changes to online courses. Tracking your progress and celebrating achievements provide effective mechanisms for sustained success.

10

Selecting Technology Tools and Approaches as Supportive Learning Mechanisms

In a considered context of learning to teach music, Colwell et al. (2017) state: 'any music teaching, whether of an individual or a group, has as its aim the development of musical independence, which consists of knowledge, good practise habits, technical proficiency, and musical understanding' (p. 48). As we seek to teach students music, the focus is on teaching, not technology. It is from this standpoint that this chapter is positioned to focus on the selection of technology tools through the lens of pedagogy first to ensure the tools themselves are supportive learning mechanisms, not the mechanisms being learned.

Pedagogy First, Technology Second

It's obvious that the year 2020 marked a year of challenge. And to be sure, it has spilled over into 2021 and beyond (Biasutti et al., 2021). As we investigated the challenges that affected many instructors, we saw research on faculty burnout (Arslan et al., 2020) and the need for increased faculty and student care (Alam, 2020; Arslan et al., 2020) come to the forefront. Examining supports that can help decrease these challenges, research has shown that those students who had high self-regulation skills prior to the 2020 pandemic were the ones that were able to successfully navigate the adoption of online assessments. Specifically, in a study by Ritchie and Sharpe (2021), findings concluded that students who chose to complete their final performance recitals in the modified form of video recording submission, rather than postpone their final recital, had higher levels of self-regulation than students who opted to wait to give a live on-location recital. Students submitting their performances via video evidenced abilities to make themselves goals to learn new technology and adjust to online submissions.

This further suggests that there needs to be specific focus on providing students with supports and scaffolded learning opportunities to teach and encourage the development of students' self-regulated learning skills within online classes. For example, incorporating a calendar tool within the LMS area of an online and providing students with assignment checklists and rubrics are mechanisms that support student self-regulation. Furthermore, including videos and links that provide explanation on music performance recordings, provide students with expectations for technology use. Providing students with examples and explanatory resources is a pedagogical approach that models expectations; the pedagogy is at the forefront.

Online music teaching supports both flexibility of learning and effective learning outcomes. Specifically, it has been shown to give students access to expert instrumental teaching without increased transportation costs (Stevens et al., 2019), convenient 24/7 access to organized content (Johnson, 2017), support cultural music performance exchanges (Hyon-Won, 2011), provide an effective mechanism to extend student care (Johnson & Merrick, 2020), and afford sustainability of classes during disasters (Klingenstein & Hagen, 2013).

Given the global focus on using technology in education, and the call to address music student anxiety and preventative injury training (Árnason et al., 2014; Perkins et al., 2017; Spahn et al., 2004) online learning approaches are posed to be strategical supports to these challenges in music conservatoria.

Guides for Choosing Technology Tools

It can be tempting to want to explore and use the latest gadget or technology tool. This 'sparkly' tool, however, may require students to learn additional technology skills, or the tool itself may underperform. Identifying approaches to effective technology tools selection can provide students with learning that is focused on learning content as opposed to technology.

Choosing Technologies

The opportunities afforded by online learning can provide students with technologies to support in-class and out-of-class learning. This means that students will likely encounter both asynchronous and synchronous technologies during their online learning. Intertwined with the fact that many technologies can be used for independent and collaborative means that we often find technologies being used in multiple ways, and sometimes beyond what their original intent.

Locating technologies that fill a teaching need can sometimes be challenging due to the vast number of options available. When choosing a technology tool to effectively support learning, it is recommended to first identify what is the learning goal to be achieved. For example, is the goal to have students independently gain conceptual knowledge out of class time, or is it to gain, and apply, conceptual knowledge out of class time. Given this scenario, it is suggested that one could consider a video for the conceptual knowledge, and H5P (i.e., HTML5 which allows for interactive video through embedded interactive questions) for supporting knowledge application. However, identifying the function, and therefore which tool, is not always obvious.

Basic Starting Tools

The technology that is required for teaching music online is constantly evolving. The instructor needs to be aware of technologies that are both reasonable in cost and the best tool for the function.

To aid in supporting how to choose effective technology tools, there are key characteristics to consider: Time; Interactivity; Collaboration; and Technology User Level. Each of these traits has options within itself that, when carefully chosen, can support the online learner.

Ruippo (2003) suggests there is a 'technical solution' (p. 2) for outlining basic technology tools for teaching music online. In his description, he suggests that teachers should use asynchronous and synchronous, as well as mono-directional and bi-directional tools. Adding to the medley of ways we use technology tools, we can add the comparison of individual and collaborative and beginner through advanced skills required. Using these attributes as categories for technology tools, we begin to force ourselves to view technology through the lens of learning support mechanisms rather than as the focused learning content. This view ensures that the technology is allowing the student to stay focused on learning the skills and discipline knowledge of music, rather than getting bogged down with a plethora of technologies. To help keep technology as a supportive learning mechanism, consider how many technology tools are used across the semester and how the tools do (or do not) relate to the class learning objectives. It is often helpful to use a graphic organizer (see Table 2) to identify how technology tools are related to the class objectives, which can in turn assist in developing an incremental plan for technology tool integration. Mapping how the technology is integrated across the semester can identify the possible challenges regarding time spent on implementing new technologies.

Table 2 Example of a Graphic Organizer to Identify Connection of Technology Tools to Class Learning Objectives.

	Learning Objective	Learning Objective	Learning Objective	Learning Objective	Learning Objective
Technology Tool Used to Support Learning Objective					
When Used in Semester (e.g., Week 2)					

Tools to Consider

- **Communicating Tools:** Email; Phone; Mail; Text; Skype; Zoom; MS Teams; LMS shells; LMS announcements; LMS Discussion boards
- **Creating Video Content:** Screencast-o-matic.com; Camtasia; Vimeo
- **Interactive Video/Game Learning:** H5P (Interactive videos, self-paced learning, and stepped out scenarios) https://h5p.org/content-types-and-applications; Twine with SugarCube (stepped out game scenarios) https://opensource.com/article/18/2/twine-gaming
- **Online Music Performing Tools:** JamKazam (live ensemble playing – https://jamkazam.com/); Sound Trap (music recording software – soundtrap.com); JackTrip (live audio and video – https://www.jacktrip.org/);
- **Music Writing Tools:** Note Flight; MuseScore; Finale; Sibelius; Flat.io; Musition; Aurelia
- **Presenting tools**: Discussion Boards; Prezi; ShowMe; Jing; PowerPoint; Keynote; Blogs; Social Network Groups; Soundcloud; YouTube; ePortfolios; StageIt; BandCamp
- **Writing Tools:** Google Docs, Discussion Forums in LMS, Dropbox, MindMeister, Evernote, WordPress

Video Journals

A helpful activity that embraces video for student learning is video journaling. During a performance class semester, students can be asked to submit a video journal activity once per week or every fortnight. The student can create a short, three-minute video that highlights their current performance ability, skills, and knowledge, as well as challenges. For example, a student could perform for two minutes in the video which is then preceded by one minute of verbal responses to specific learning questions as created by the teacher. Questions like, 'What is an area that you are having most challenges with this week?' Or, identify two or three musicians or ensembles you listen to this week. The use of specific questions for students to answer highlights expected activities that students should be addressing each week. This type of questioning also helps support students to learn helpful reflective questions and further their overall self-regulation skills. Encouraging the students to listen to their own video prior to submitting the recording journal also supports further student reflection.

Students can understand the effectiveness of hearing and seeing video content through a video response by the teacher. If the instructor uses video response to the student's video journal, students often remark on how effective and efficient it is for improving practice. Students are able to watch the asynchronous video at a convenient and flexible time as well as re-watch and pause the video to carefully take in the instructor's feedback and suggestions. Demonstration of posture, instrument technique, breath support, and a myriad of other key skills and components is items to be shared by the instructor to the student through a video response.

Online Student Practice Rooms

A supportive community learning approach can include the use of Zoom rooms for practising and providing peer feedback. The objective of these types of collaborative activities should focus on positive and supportive information that will help students improve in their musicianship.

Example 1: In small groups of two, students can perform for each other, or if one student is muted, they can perform duets. Once students have played together, they can give each other peer feedback. Students unfamiliar with this type of exercise may need exemplars or questions to guide them in giving effective critical peer feedback.

Example 2: In small groups of three to five students, students can enter an online video conference space and take time to perform for each other. Alternatively, students can use this time as focused practice time where in all students are on mute with videos on. For some students, this is a helpful accountability mechanism.

Learning the creative art of music requires a supportive teacher and appropriate assessments or learning tasks. Teaching music online adds an additional layer of complexity. The shift to online learning due to Covid-19 found many tertiary music instructors quickly adopting online music assessments. Transitioning to teach and assess music students online requires an understanding of assessment alignment to learning objectives as well as appropriate technology adoption. While it is not expected for an entire conservatorium to move all subjects online, there is a need to demonstrate both agility and technology adoption for the purposes of inclusive education (e.g., Universal Design for Learning [UDL] opportunities of video, text, and audio), curriculum differentiation (i.e., addressing student-based learning needs), and musically supportive assessment and feedback mechanisms when teaching music online. Given this context, understanding the degree to which specific online music assessments meet associated student learning outcomes becomes necessary to support programme quality.

However, as one example, less than 15 per cent of Australian university music programmes offered online music learning prior to January 2020 (Johnson & Cheok, forthcoming). This is significantly lower when compared to over 40 per cent of American's National Association of Schools of Music (NASM) institutions offering online music classes in 2015 (Johnson, 2021; Johnson & Hawley, 2017). Australian universities, and universities worldwide are preparing to provide students with long-term solutions for Covid-19 learning – fully online classes are no longer optional. The discipline of music has not been immune to this shift to a fully online teaching paradigm. The abrupt shift to transition music classes to an online environment was felt considerably not only by Australia's music students, but the entire world, as their teachers looked to move their music teaching online.

However, does the 'lift and shift' of music teaching from its face-to-face model to an online version represent an equitable learning approach? Often, technology is used as a mediator to help further student learning. Research studies have identified that the use of technology is an effective tool to support student development of music knowledge and skills (Keast, 2009; Webster, 2011). Further, online learning research indicates that providing students with content that is aligned to the UDL framework supports diversity of learning approaches (Rose & Meyer, 2002). Merging the fields of music and online learning, we find that there are various studies that highlight online music assessments available that have been used at the tertiary music level (Alcorn, 2018; Eremenko et al., 2020; Keast, 2009; Lierse, 2015).

Students First

Studies concerning music students suggest the implementation of emotional and psychological support services (Perkins et al., 2017), in addition to preventative training of musculoskeletal injuries in musicians (Árnason et al., 2014), and healthy practices routines (Perkins et al., 2017), is necessary for conservatoire students. Faced with fixed performance deadlines and finite practice times arranged within a full schedule of music classes, music students experience stress and performance anxiety at a different pace and level than most university-level students.

Through semi-structured interviews with UK conservatoire students (n=20), Perkins et al. (2017) suggested students perceive barriers within the conservatoire to include: lifestyle challenges, practice and learning challenges, low levels of health awareness, psychological distress, challenges with performance feedback, and workload, among others. The results further indicate a 'need for continued work to embed health and well-being support as an integral component … [and] "provide spaces for *learning* performance … allowing students to connect with the aspects of performance that sustain well-being while minimizing the negative implication"' (p. 13).

In a study comparing music students to its other University of Freiburg faculties, Spahn et al. (2004) reported, 'Music students rated 8.4% in the HADS depression scale, and 33.5% on the anxiety scale, which was significantly more than the other students and placed them in the borderline or elevated range' (p. 26). Indeed, music conservatoires are at key junctures wherein addressing these health and well-being are not optional but necessary for the health of musicians, and for the integrous sustainability of the conservatoire. Findings suggest there is 'a need for more radical scrutiny of the cultures of conservatoires and an assessment of how these can be modified to best optimize students' health and well-being' (Perkins et al., 2017, p. 1).

These students also have requirements to attend in-class lectures and music lessons, participate in multiple weekly rehearsals, and perform semester technical exams. Music students often spend time commuting to school, work to support their schooling, and/or have carer responsibilities. Together with the need to develop an entrepreneurial mindset for the known circuitous route of the entrepreneurial musician (Johnson et al., 2019), music students are often time poor which adds to their overall challenges to health and well-being. However, research has identified online learning as an equal alternative to face-to-face learning. Studies in online music learning have evidenced positive music learning outcomes in both online music lessons (Dye, 2007) and online music tertiary subjects (Damon & Rockinson-Szapkiw, 2018).

Using Technology to Develop Community

One of the exciting aspects in online music teaching is the opportunity to engage with students no matter where they are located. However, it can be challenging to establish community online without careful and considered approach to creating an online presence.

Online presence is not merely appearing on a Zoom screen and talking. It is about making connections and community through active participation activities.

From the research of (Park and Bonk, 2007), we learn that students in an online course need to feel connected to their instructor and peers within the first two weeks of their online course. If students do not connect during this time, they will generally decline in course motivation and activity overall. Given the importance of this initial time frame, instructors need to look for purposeful ways to develop community across the student body at the onset of an online course. In a practical sense, one could even suggest that the organized sending of a welcome email prior to the start of class is part of the development of an online class community. Further, the inclusion of instructor contact, email, and even a video welcome can go far in providing that initial first step in establishing community.

Thinking through the importance of scaffolding and structuring the online environment for clarity and intuitive design, it is reasonable to suggest that design can influence how a student chooses to interact or not interact in an online course. Therefore, the fostering of community is also connected to course design. Seeking opportunities to include activities that allow students to engage in multiple ways is at the forefront. This means creating activities like introduction discussion areas, student cafes, and collaborative projects across the class semester. Using technology to further develop community, we can see that the addition of video can further support the fostering of community. For example, an introduction discussion can welcome students to use a video recording of their introduction rather than merely typing their introduction.

Finally, establishing an online presence can also be supported by the modelling of effective communication practices by the instructor. As musicians, we know

Selecting Technology Tools and Approaches as Supportive Learning Mechanisms 155

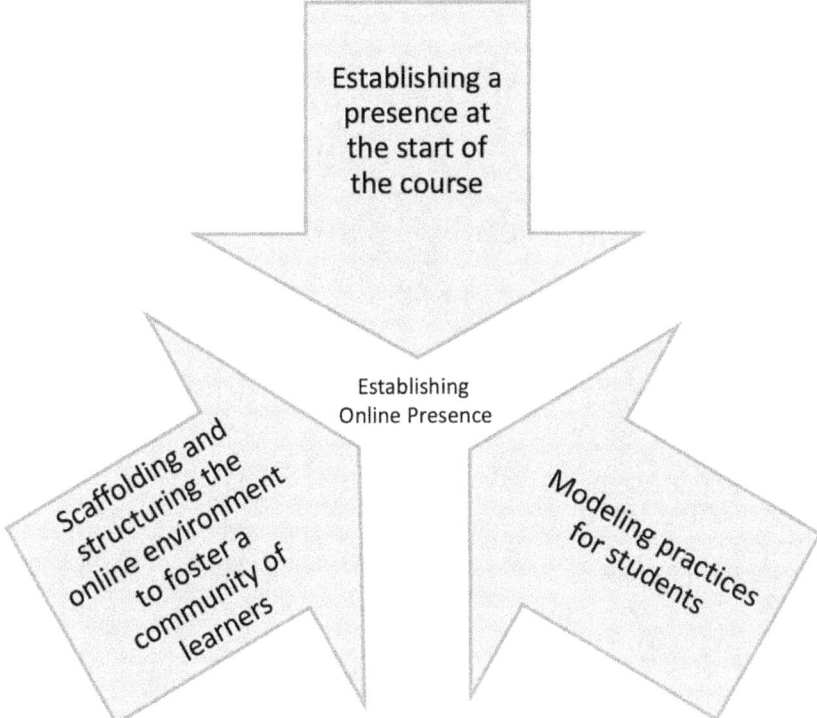

Figure 15 Establishing Online Presence.

the value of modelling for expert musicianship. In the case of community, instructors will want to model effective approaches for communication that they want their students in turn to use.

From these three key elements (i.e., establishing presence at the start of the course, scaffolding and structuring to foster a community of learners, and modelling practices for students) students will be able to understand the importance of engagement and have opportunity for themselves to establish their online presence in your online class. Figure 15 provides a visual on how these elements come together to support establishing online presence.

Part Three

Future Innovations

The final section of the book focuses on how readers can continue to improve their knowledge, skills, and networks for continued improvement. There is a focus on the importance of being part of a community of learning and sharing our knowledge with each other to improve our field of teaching music online.

11

Sharing Our Knowledge

Importance of Knowledge Sharing

It is clear that we are still in the nascent stages of learning effective online music teaching practices and strategies. With the limited exploration and practice of online music teaching prior to the 2020 pandemic, researchers explored the higher-level research questions regarding efficacy, effective teaching strategies, and overall differences between learning music face-to-face or online. The quick shift to teaching music online in higher education in 2020 provided additional classes, instructors, and music topics to be explored in online music research.

With the increased use of online meetings and conferences, researchers have found themselves connecting more often with their global research community. This means that there is more opportunity to share and research on the new practice is developing in online music learning. Ease of communication has allowed for further exploration and increased opportunities to locate voluntary participants for extended research in online music teaching and learning. This can result in an increase of research projects, outputs, and publications in what was once a niche area of research.

Technology use in university-level music teaching is often dependent on the receptive climate of academic staff. While not as prevalent as other practical-based disciplines, university-level music classes in the UK are steadily seeing increased use of technology (Waddell & Willamon, 2019) and evidence an exponential rate of increase in adopting online music classes at the Bachelor levels in the United States since 2021 (Johnson, 2017, 2021). However, countries, like Australia, are still lagging in technology adoption for music classes (Crawford, 2013; Johnson & Cheok, forthcoming). Prior to the 2020 pandemic, teaching music online at the tertiary level was not yet prevalent across undergraduate and graduate programmes as highlighted in a global review of the synchronous online music learning by Lisboa et al. (2022). However, there are scholars that have been involved in this area of study across the globe.

As instructors in online music teaching, we have opportunity to explore research in effective approaches to teaching music online, the development of new and improved technology tools for teaching music online, and the identification of future trends beyond the pandemic. By creating communities that are open to sharing researched informed practices we will be able to further advance music education.

The financial challenges facing many conservatoires in schools of music post pandemic are a reality. By coming together and sharing knowledge we may be able to collectively support the sustaining of music education across generations. Considerations for international collaborations, grant projects, and cross-institutional teaching maybe more feasible in a post-Covid-19 world with a broader openness for online teaching.

Ways to Share Knowledge

There are many ways to share our research knowledge in online music teaching. From our small institutional academic groupings to large online conference events, technology can support effective approaches to bring together small and large communities for knowledge sharing.

Knowledge sharing can include the use of social media. Following researchers' and online music teachers' Twitter accounts can be an effective approach to learning research-informed online teaching practices. Furthermore, the use of Facebook groups, podcasts, and other social media groups can support the sharing of ideas with like-minded educators.

Take time to consider how you can explore the area of online music teaching and share your experiences with other online music instructors.

The following section identifies specific authors and articles in relation to teaching music online. This is not an exhaustive listing. Feel free to connect with the author to have additional topics and citations shared through an online resource webpage. Visit the author's personal website (http://research.carolj.net) for updated listings.

Online Music Technology Tools

Anderson, A., & Northcote, M. (2018). Australian Studies of Videoconference and Video-Assisted Instrumental Music Teaching: What Have We Learned? *Australian Journal of Music Education, 52*(1), 3–18.

Crawford, R. (2013). Evolving Technologies Require Educational Policy Change: Music Education for the 21st Century. *Australasian Journal of Educational Technology*, *29*(5), 717–734. https://doi.org/10.14742/ajet.268.

Ørngreen, R., Levinsen, K., Buhl, M., Solak, T., Jakobsen, M., & Andersen, J. (2012). Videoconferencing in Music Education at the Conservatory Level. In *Designs for Learning 2012, 3rd International Conference Exploring Learning Environments, 25-27 April 2012, Copenhagen, Denmark: Conference Proceedings* (pp. 133-135). Retrieved from http://pure.au.dk/portal/files/45188015/DfL2012_Conference_Proceedings.pdf

Veblen, K. K., Kruse, N. B., Messenger, S. J., & Letain, M. (2018). Children's Clapping Games on the Virtual Playground. *International Journal of Music Education*, *36*(4), 547–559. https://doi.org/10.1177%2F0255761418772865.

Online Music Pedagogy

Johnson, C. (2017). Teaching Music Online: Changing Pedagogical Approach When Moving to the Online Environment. *London Review of Education*, *15*(3), 439–466. https://doi.org/10.18546/LRE.15.3.08.

Pike, P. D. (2017). Improving Music Teaching and Learning through Online Service: A Case Study of a Synchronous Online Teaching Internship. *International Journal of Music Education*, *35*(1), 107–117. https://doi.org/10.1177/2F0255761415613534.

Online Composition Pedagogy

Biasutti, M., & Concina, E. (2021). Online Composition: Strategies and Processes during Collaborative Electroacoustic Composition. *British Journal of Music Education*, *38*(1), 58-73. https://doi.org/10.1017/S0265051720000157.

Music History

Keast, D. A. (2009). A Constructivist Application for Online Learning in Music. *Research and Issues in Music Education*, *7*(1), 1–8.

Scarnati, B., & Garcia, P. (2008). The Fusion of Learning Theory and Technology in an Online Music History Course Redesign. *Innovate: Journal of Online Education*, *4*(2). Retrieved from https://nsuworks.nova.edu/innovate/vol4/iss2/4.

Music Appreciation

Kang, Y., & Ritzhaupt, A. (2021). A Comparative Study of Game-Based Online Learning in Music Appreciation: An Analysis of Student Motivation and Achievement. *Journal of Educational Multimedia and Hypermedia, 30*(1), 59–80. Retrieved from https://ufdc.ufl.edu/UFE0051450/00001.

Online Music Performance

Alpiste Penalba, F., Rojas-Rajs, T., Lorente, P., Iglesias, F., Fernández, J., & Monguet, J. (2013). A Telepresence Learning Environment for Opera Singing: Distance Lessons Implementations over Internet2. *Interactive Learning Environments, 21*(5), 438–455. https://doi.org/10.1080/10494820.2011.584322.

Biasutti, M., Antonini Philippe, R., & Schiavio, A. (2021). Assessing Teachers' Perspectives on Giving Music Lessons Remotely during the COVID-19 Lockdown Period. *Musicae Scientiae*, 1029864921996033. https://doi.org/10.1177/1029864921996033.

Blackburn, A. (2017). Performing Online: Approaches to Teaching Performance Studies in Higher Education within a Fully Online Environment. *Australian Journal of Music Education, 51*(1), 63–72.

Cameron, A. (2007), *Evaluation of the 'Instrumental Tuition by Video Conferencing' (ITVC) Project in Dumfries & Galloway Schools*. Executive Summary. Warwick University.

Juntunen, Pirkko. (2011). Music Technology in Finnish String Instrument and Orchestra Instruction. *Fourth International Journal of Intercultural Arts Education: Design Learning and Well-Being*. 97–114.

Levinsen, K. T., Ørngreen, R., Buhl, M., Jakobsen, M. L., & Andersen, J. (2011). Instrumental Distance Learning in Higher Music Education. In *10th European Conference on e-learning, Academic Publishing Limited* (pp. 993–996). Virtual Learning Environments in Spain. *European Journal of Open, Distance and E-Learning, 1*.

Constructivism and Online Teaching

Keast, D. A. (2009). A Constructivist Application for Online Learning in Music. *Research and Issues in Music Education, 7*(1).

Online Community for Music Learning

Adams, K. (2021). Research to Resource: Developing a Sense of Community in Online Learning Environments. *Update: Applications of Research in Music Education, 39*(2), 5–9. https://doi.org/10.1177%2F8755123320943985.

Bayley, J. G., & Waldron, J. (2020). 'It's Never Too Late': Adult Students and Music Learning in One Online and Offline Convergent Community Music School. *International Journal of Music Education, 38*(1), 36–51. https://doi.org/10.1177%2F0255761419861441.

Kenny, A. (2013). 'The Next Level': Investigating Teaching and Learning within an Irish Traditional Music Online Community. *Research Studies in Music Education, 35*(2), 239–253. http://doi.org/10.1177/1321103X13508349.

Waldron, J. (2011). Locating Narratives in Postmodern Spaces: A Cyber Ethnographic Field Study of Informal Music Learning in Online Community. *Action, Criticism, and Theory for Music Education, 10*(2), 32–60.

Waldron, J. (2013). User-Generated Content, YouTube and Participatory Culture on the Web: Music Learning and Teaching in Two Contrasting Online Communities. *Music Education Research, 15*(3), 257–274. http://doi.org/10.1080/14613808.2013.772131.

Authenticity

Schmidt-Jones, C. (2017). Offering Authentic Learning Activities in the Context of Open Resources and Real-World Goals: A Study of Self-Motivated Online Music Learning. *European Journal of Open, Distance and E-Learning, 20*(1), 111–125. http://doi.org/10.1515/eurodl-2017-0007.

Online Music Performance

Koutsoupidou, T. (2014). Online Distance Learning and Music Training: Benefits, Drawbacks and Challenges. *Open Learning, 29*(3), 243–255. http://doi.org/10.12681/icodl.536.

Online Presence

Dunlap, J. C., Verma, G., & Johnson, H. L. (2016). Presence+Experience: A Framework for the Purposeful Design of Presence in Online Courses. *TechTrends: Linking Research and Practice to Improve Learning, 60*(2), 145–151. http://doi.org/10.1007/s11528-016-0029-4.

Where Is Next?

One of the main challenges in online music teaching is the aspect of performing together at the same time. The challenges of latency as well as clarity of audio create difficulty in ensuring an effective online music performance class. However, there are opportunities to creatively take up new approaches to teaching music online (e.g., see Figure 16), try out new forms of online assessment activities (e.g., see Figure 17), as well as explore how online music performance classes can take place using improved or new technologies (e.g., JackTrip, Real Time Audio, and others).

When exploring dual mode teaching, there are opportunities for performance-based learning to take place in both the on-campus ensemble group and the online group. Through the use of traditional, face-to-face ensemble playing, students in the on-campus class can easily perform together (see Figure 16. Synchronous Music Activities in Dual-Mode Teaching).

In the online class, the creation of breakout rooms, with dyad or duet groupings, can support music performance learning outcomes of self-reflection, self-regulation, and developing performance listening skills. For example, in a dyad grouping, one student can be nominated as the solo performer and the other student nominated as a duet player. With her microphone on, the solo performer transmits her performance to the other duet player in the breakout room. Focusing on solo performance skills that include self-assessment of sound, articulation, musical expression, and tempo, the soloist can involve herself in focused performance practice routines. Alternately, given the opportunity to play along with the soloist, the muted duet player is able to listen to herself

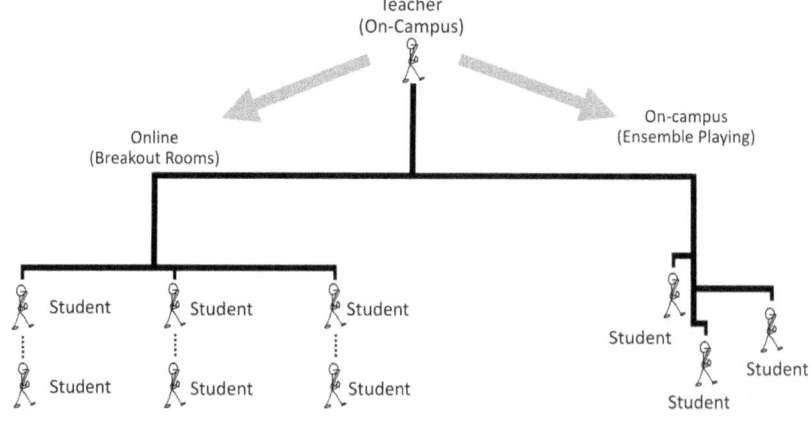

Figure 16 Synchronous Music Activities in Dual-Mode Teaching.

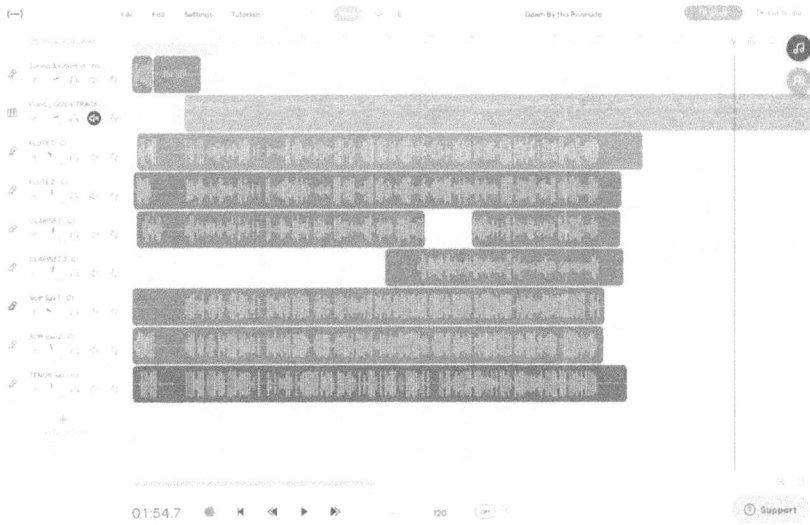

Figure 17 Asynchronous Ensemble Recording Activity Using SoundTrap.

play as a duet and focus on her ensemble performance skills (e.g., playing together, intonation skills, and overall musical expression). These two learning episodes take place at the same time yet provide students with different learning outcomes. Researching the efficacy of breakout room soloist and duet practices can surface specific routines and skills that are furthered in this dynamic learning environment.

Online Music Assessment

We discussed earlier that students desire dynamic feedback in their learning (see Chapter 6). From this standpoint, it can be understood that the online music student would find video feedback useful in their learning as well. However, in terms of video and audio feedback use in online classes, and more specifically online music classes, there is still a need for more research. Currently, this research area has surfaced anecdotal information and requires further investigation. Therefore, it would be helpful to have future studies explore the efficacy of asynchronous video feedback for online music students. That is, understanding the degree to which visual clarity of the instructor and instructor's instrument is needed for the student, to what extent the instructor should perform on her instrument in the feedback, as well as explore research that examines the effective technology tools and peripherals that would best support the creation of video feedback.

Artificial Intelligence and Machine Learning

The area of artificial intelligence (AI) and machine learning has become a playground for exploring AI sonic artforms, music composition, music notation integration, and much more. These technological advancements have implications for teaching music online. The development of AI apps for music learning is already influencing how students use their practice time and extend their music theory knowledge. As we continue into the future, it will be important to identify ways in which AI can positively enhance music student learning, practises for teaching, and supporting music instructor professional development.

Specifically, the use of AI for supporting online music assessment maybe a reasonable innovation in a not so distant future. With the ability for AI to administer and evaluate second language assessments, similar software engines could be used to evaluate tones and their alignment to a notated musical score. This type of innovation could have ramifications for solutionizing the problems of incorrect musical practice across all levels of players and performers.

3D Music Performance

It is not unrealistic to highlight the advancement of hologram technology and the possibilities it has for music performance and music learning. With the greatest challenge of online music teaching focusing often on the limited visual of the entire student and teacher, their exploration of hologram technology may provide a legitimate solution to teaching music across distances. With current practices of music performances including the use of hologram technologies, a reasonable expectation includes the advancement for use in music teaching and learning.

The advances in online music teaching using synchronous technologies have proven that music learning has no boundaries. This suggests that there may be additional opportunities to explore beyond our institutional walls. For example, the exploration of community music programmes, aged care facilities, hospital networks, and more, may be opportune areas for public engagement with online music teaching and learning. Bridging the gap between secondary music classes and university instructors, music teaching can now be easily negotiated through online means. Invited lectures, special music performances, and cultural exchanges are just some of the many opportunities that we can navigate in our online offerings.

You Are a Future Innovator

As we continue to explore innovation in online music teaching and learning, we should consider ourselves as possible innovators. Reaching beyond our regular realm of teaching, we have opportunity to influence and impact the practice of music teaching. While this may seem a daunting task, purposeful advancement and improvement in our own teaching can lead to broader innovations.

We are all encouraged to consider new approaches and technologies to enhance and support online music teaching and learning. If we incorporate one more advancement, or create one more video, we are changing our teaching practice in a progressive manner. The exploration of one new teaching practice per semester by each one of us provides a reasonable approach to ensuring the advancement of music education overall – one step at a time.

12

Creating Professional Learning Networks

Introduction

Awareness of effective teaching approaches and technologies can help keep our teaching current and fresh. Therefore, this chapter highlights opportunities availed by informal and formal learning opportunities. One of the notable outcomes from the research and case studies is the importance of mentorship. Mentorship, unlike coaching, provides the mentee with opportunity to have proactive and in-depth discussion with a mentor. While a mentor is not expected to provide answers, mentorship discussions often support the exploration of self-reflection and different approaches of inquiry into problems, challenges, and philosophical viewpoints to surface answers within the mentee. While coaching focuses on a coach guiding someone through a specific process or activity, mentorship is open to probing concepts and ideas in multiple ways to help the mentee locate the best solution for her unique scenario.

Given the communication focus with the discipline of music itself, mentoring programmes should address the specificity of the cultural music context, along with practical, technical, and pedagogical issues found within the online environment.

Case study three had a number of instructors that identified the use of mentoring in their online teaching journey. This process was found invaluable. Not only was it a time for the mentee to ask questions and probe for alternative solutions, but the process was also found to be one that could be 'passed on'. That is, those that were mentored also mentored others. This cyclical nature of mentorship has been identified as a supportive outcome in the adoption of innovations in teaching contexts (Johnson & Cooper, 2013). Starting with only a mentor and one mentee, there is opportunity for exponential impact as the mentee becomes a mentor, whose mentees become mentors, and so on. Mentorships can form from informal peer connections, as well as from more formal professional learning communities.

Communities of Practice

As we look to our future in teaching with technology and more specifically teaching music online, we see that there is a need to have a posture for lifelong learning. Whether you are at the beginning of your music teaching career, or if you have taught music for a long time, surrounding yourself with others who have similar interests in music teaching and improving teaching practice are keys to lifelong learning.

Lifelong learning does not take place alone. While we can attend a variety of classes, workshops, or explore self-directed learning resources, learning, like music, is a social action. Another way to take part in lifelong learning is through the exploration of a Community of Practice (CoP). Coined by Lave and Wenger (1991), a CoP is a group of people bounded by a shared practice that come together to learn and exchange ideas (e.g., engagement) about improving their practice across an extended period of time. Built on formal or informal group membership, a CoP may be a band, peer group, colleague-based work group, professional organization, etc.

Generally, a CoP involves members that have a shared interest or passion in a particular practice, such as teaching music. Over an extended time and specified place (Wenger, 1998), members regularly take part in formal or informal community connections through the sharing of knowledge about a particular practice. This exchange can happen in a face-to-face or online delivery mode (i.e., synchronous or asynchronous formats). Together, members experience a sense of belonging to the group through the identification of a similar practice and/or interest.

Belonging to a CoP has been identified as a supportive mechanism to foster resilience during times of organizational and learning challenges (Brown & Duguid, 1991). Group members find support through the connections of ideas, social exchange, and transfer of knowledge among group members.

One of the key outcomes of a CoP is the knowledge exchange that takes place between members. That is, it is a community formed around learning with members committed to sharing their knowledge with the community. Visualized as three concentric spheres by Wenger-Trayner and Wenger-Trayner (2015), the primary characteristics of a CoP include: domain, community, and practice. That is, an identified domain of interest and concern, members commitment to actively sharing of ideas and knowledge together, and a definitive area of practitioner scope, knowledge, and resources. A community of musical practice is often the term used to describe a CoP for 'a group of people who form a community of practice through music making and/or musical interest' (Kenny, 2016, p. 16).

The importance of taking part in a community of practice for online music teachers is so that there can be a community that shares knowledge, skills, and resources for teaching music online. This may mean that some may look to their university or institution to take part in a community of practice or for others this may mean starting a CoP with those interested in learning or advancing their knowledge on teaching music online. Since a CoP is not defined by a formal or informal membership, in a CoP there is opportunity for all levels of practitioners, both new and not so new, to be involved. Together, members take part in sharing, exchanging, and advancing knowledge in the field.

As members share and learn about the practice of teaching music online, members build practitioner skills as well as leadership skills. In his research, Kenny reported that shared leadership, problem solving, roles assumed, participation and enjoyment all help to characterize the process of building a 'community of musical practice' (p. 396). The development and participation in a CoP in teaching music online not only impacts members directly involved in the CoP, but can influence the broader community, institution, and organizations ancillary or directly connected to its members.

The creation of a CoP involves four key elements: determination of membership (e.g., Who can be a member?; Is it a formal or informal community membership?); regularity of membership involvement (e.g., When do members exchange ideas?); identification of a protocol or procedure for sharing of knowledge, skills, and/or resources (e.g., How is learning shared?); and identification of facilitator(s) (e.g., Who is responsible for leading and/or guiding the community to ensure continuance of focus?). These four elements uphold the focus of the CoP which supports the development of meaningful connections for CoP members. The identification of boundaries and the expectations of the CoP and its members encourage a healthy and sustainable community.

It is also important to remember that the duration of a CoP is not a predefined requisite – CoPs may only exist for a limited period of time. In his Stages of Development, Wenger (1998) suggests that there are five identifiable stages that a community of practice exhibits across its lifetime: Potential, Coalescing, Active, Dispersed, and Memorable. The first stage, *potential*, is the discovery stage wherein people begin to come together through common situations. In the second stage, *coalescing*, there is a realized benefit for coming together as a community of members. This leads to the third stage, *active*, wherein members are actively engaging in the sharing of practice resources and community. When a community of practice experiences a decline in intensity or wain in need for engagement, the COP can be described at the fourth stage, *Dispersed*. At this stage, members may keep in touch with each other, however activity is minimal, and the community may only serve as a knowledge source. In the final stage, *memorable*, the community is referred to only as a past entity or memorable connection. The length of time a CoP spends in each of these stages can be impacted by the community, its members, and its interest topic.

As you continue in your teaching career, identify two or three possible communities of practice that may be of interest to you. It might be a community band, a local music teachers' organization or a national conference. Find one that interests you and supports you as a lifelong leaner.

For example, a CoP focused on teaching music online is the annual *Teaching Music in Higher Education* conference (www.teachingmusiconlineinhighered.com). Convened by Dr Carol Johnson and Dr Brad Merrick, the annual online conference grew out of a small gathering of peers to share ideas on research and practices around teaching music online. One of the main focuses of the group is the opportunity for practitioners and research practitioners to exchange and reflect on innovative and contemporary teaching within the area of online music teaching. Open to those practitioners in higher education music teaching, members in this community of practice participate in the annual conference and return to their institutions where they share the knowledge that they have learned from other members.

Communities of musical practice are identified across the research literature. Researchers have explored these communities in terms of music teacher training (Ilari, 2010; Pelligrino et al., 2018), musical styles (Hewitt, 2009), virtual and online music communities (Bernard et al., 2018; Waldron, 2009, 2018) in addition to many other communities of musical practice.

Current Landscape of Using Online Teaching for Music Learning

Technology use in university-level music teaching is often dependent on the climate of receptibility of academic staff. While not as prevalent as other practical-based disciplines, university-level music classes in the UK are steadily seeing increased use of technology (Waddell & Williamon, 2019) and evidence an exponential rate of increase in adopting online music classes at the Bachelor levels in the United States since 2012 (Johnson, 2021). However, Australia is still lagging in technology adoption for music classes (Crawford, 2013) – and teaching music online at the tertiary level is not yet prevalent across Australia's undergraduate and graduate programmes (Johnson & Cheok, forthcoming).

The complexities involved in decision-making to implement online classes and learning approaches in conservatoires are vast. The effectiveness of student learning outcomes from taking a class online versus face-to-face is proven as similar or more effective in core curricula, STEM-based disciplines (Cook et al., 2008). Scholars suggest that online learning approaches have the 'potential benefit of instilling deeper learning of topics by virtue of repeated and convenient access to content presented in a range of media' (Bhatti et al., 2011, p. 459). This personalized learning approach is commonly advocated in practical, traditional apprentice-style disciplines, such as surgery (Bhatti et al., 2011), dentistry (Schönwetter et al., 2010), and physio in universities (Hossain et al., 2015).

In today's technology-based climate, it is common for university students to have at least one, if not more, online class during their degree of studies (Seaman et al., 2018). Music, and the conservatoire in general, is beginning to add online class offerings at the undergraduate and graduate levels. Prior to 2020, studies showed a steady increase in online music class offerings for university-level music students (Groulx & Hernly, 2010; Johnson, 2017) in the United States. However, given the notable positive well-being outcomes arising from the availability of online options and the high rate of music student psychological distress as outlined above, it is suggested that the adoption of online learning approaches could provide supportive mechanisms for overall student well-being.

There is a distinct gap in adoption of online learning approaches for music students versus the STEM disciplines. While there are complex administrative decisions when considering the adoption of online learning approaches into higher education music learning, it is reasonable to observe from the broader academic offerings that online learning can, and is, a support mechanism for student well-being.

Online music teaching has provided its students with flexibility of time for job and carer responsibilities (Damon & Rockinson-Szapkiw, 2018), support for students through content organization (Johnson, 2017), cultural online music exchanges (Hyon-Won, 2011; McAlpine, 2020), accessibility for learners with disabilities (Merck & Johnson, 2017), and sustainability of classes during disasters (Klingenstein & Hagen, 2013). These are just a few explicit examples that demonstrate how online music learning can support students into the post-pandemic era and perhaps concurrently address the well-known challenges of music student anxiety and preventative injury training (Arnason, 2014; Perkins et al., 2017; Spahn et al., 2004). Additionally, policies that support how students can have a voice to choose their on- or off-campus learning modalities are necessary strategic considerations for conservatoria leadership.

Global Research Projects in Teaching Music Online

Many scholars have addressed the use of distance learning, or online learning, in music across various countries. Ruippo (2003) highlighted the use of ICT distance technology for music learning at Finland's Sibelius Academy in 1996 while Stevens et al. (2019) explored online music tuition use and technological set-up to rural areas of Victoria, Australia. The UK's Connect ReSound project (King et al., 2019) further identified student learning outcomes through remote community tuition across rural areas in the UK. The challenges and benefits of networked music performance across European conservatoires were the focus of the Erasmus+ INTERMusic project (Delle Monache et al., 2022). Finally, the Canadian MusicGrid Project study by Masum et al. (2005) provided online violin lessons to the remote area of Kangiqsuallujuaq, Quebec, in Canada. While these projects were not specific to higher education, together they signify the global need of music tuition in remote communities and the search for pedagogical approaches to effectively implement online teaching for music.

To help support you in your specific area of online music teaching, consider exploring the research of some of the identified scholars in outlined in Table 3.

Currently, there are a number of international music conservatoires that are implementing online music classes to support their students (Lisboa et al., 2022). Institutions such as Milan Conservatoire 'G Verdi', Royal Danish Academy of Music (RDAM), and Trinity Laban Conservatoire in London are offering online classes to ensure their students are able to take part in music learning across large distances. Furthermore, large grant organizations have contributed funding towards the development of online music resources to share between multiple conservatoires (Delle Monache et al., 2019). However, as these performance-based specialist programmes seek to develop online resources, there is an understanding of the importance of the resource, yet a gap regarding where they fit in within the overarching delivery for effective online music

Table 3 Scholars Writing on the Topic of Online Music Teaching According to Country.

Scholar	Topic Area	Country
Biasutti, Michele	Pedagogical strategies; online composition	Italy
Blackburn, Alana	Teaching performance studies online	Australia
Brändström, Wiklund, & Lundström, 2012	Technology tools for teaching music online	Sweden
Cameron, Alan	Video streaming for music education	Scotland
Chafe, Chris	JackTrip; low latency networks for music	United States
Dammers, Richard	Online applied music lessons	United States
Della-Monache, Stefano	Networked music performance	Italy
Johnson, Carol	Online music pedagogy; historical timeline of online music teaching	Australia and Canada
Keast, Dan	Constructivist online music learning	United States
King, Andrew	Connect Resound Project; rural music teaching	England
Koutsoupidou, Theano	Online distance learning in music	Greece
Levinsen, K. T. and Buhl, M.	Video conferencing and music	Denmark
Pike, Pamela	Online graduate piano pedagogy	United States
Rofe, Michael	Online Orchestra Telematic music performance	England
Ruippo, Matti	Distance learning in music	Finland
Ruthmann, Alex	Online collaborative music tools	United States
Stevens, Robin	Distance instrumental music tuition	Australia
Ward, Frances	Virtual music pedagogies	Ireland

teaching. While it is important, and costly, to develop the learning resources, it is of equal importance to know where and how they fit into an online learning approach for music.

Professional Learning Networks

The use of professional learning networks can be helpful in supporting both the advancement of our teaching expertise and the overall music profession. When we consider the importance of networks, we understand that the learning interactions that happened across individual, group, and cultural levels help form our identity and roles in contemporary learning connections that we make through professional development networks are in themselves microcultures. These small cultures in themselves define particular professional norms and behaviours within the group. This suggests how the influence of one person, a small group of people, or a community of professionals can impact and influence a profession.

As we meet colleagues at conferences, in our hallways, and in video conferences, we have opportunity to learn from each other. Sharing a wedge of knowledge and expertise and being open to learning from others create a positive and inviting learning culture.

Professional networks are communities of individuals that often form through institutional, corporate, or individual initiatives. The social constructivist experience of the network allows for the explicit use of reflection, dialogue, and discourse among the group members. While each professional network is unique in its core makeup, the essence of involvement for meaningful learning is the desired outcome. Successful professional networks have individuals that are constantly engaging in self-monitoring and sensemaking as they seek to further their own understanding of their topic area. Meaningful discourse often starts with the collaborative learning process; Individuals share ideas, activities, and approaches with each other.

Successful professional learning networks themselves include key learning elements; they often outline clear impractical descriptions of how to connect to the larger social group. With the incorporation of technology, online professional learning networks can be found as small microcultures that form on Twitter feeds, Facebook groups, and other social media. It's not the tool itself; it is how we CHOOSE to engage within our network.

Professional learning networks are integral parts of our professional development. Giving time to take part in professional development through a professional learning network can be a rewarding learning experience of learning through community. From this perspective, as we grow our expertise in online music learning, so too should we grow in our sharing and learning across our professional learning networks.

Conclusion

While online learning presents considerable assistance for many learners and has evidenced to hold considerable equality in learning outcomes to that of the traditional classroom (Tallent-Runnels et al., 2006), the merging of music education and online learning does have a variety of possible challenges to overcome.

This merging of technology and tradition could possess the following challenges: faculty acceptance to use of technology and training; time constraints for developing of online music education courses and programmes; administration and policy evaluation and assessment; and technological inconsistencies such as lack of high-bandwidth internet access for students and/or instructors. While many of these challenges are secondary-level phenomenon (i.e., personal challenges or views), the subject of adequate internet access is a primary, and essential requirement for execution of online learning.

This last challenge is one that is specific to the global outcome of online music education. While online music education is generally feasible in developed nations, the availability of post-secondary online music performance education for geographically isolated students may be impeded by technology itself. As Cox (2006) states:

> We need more research that will illuminate our understanding of music education's function in fostering a sense of identities that have to be constantly invented, transformed, and recovered. The result of such investigation should serve to encourage music educators to question aspects of their own music education tradition that they may take for granted.
>
> (pp. 79–80)

Perhaps it is within this context that authentic online music teaching will not only be made available to support music education to the masses, but to provide opportunity for music teachers to further innovate, invent, transform, and recover music education for sustainable music education for generations to come.

Glossary

Asynchronous: Something that happens outside of a specific time. For example, if an activity is asynchronous, it means that one student can participate at 6 am in the morning, and another student can participate equitably at 6 pm.

Case Study: Case study is the method of research that identifies a single, bounded phenomenon for social sciences study that is composed of human phenomena of social exchanges and events (Merriam, 2002; Miles, Hubberman, & Saldaña, 2014; Yin, 2014).

Cognitive presence: Cognitive presence is a term used within the Community of Inquiry framework (Arbaugh et al., 2008). This measurement identifies the extent to which student engages within the online environment through application and exchange of learning information.

Community of Inquiry Framework (COI): Developed by Garrison, Anderson, and Archer (2001), this framework outlines how teaching presence, social presence, and cognitive present intersect in the online environment for effective learning outcomes.

Dual-Mode Teaching: Instruction wherein the instructor is teaching from the classroom, with students taking part from both the physical classroom with the teacher and with student joining in via online. This experience happens in real time (i.e., synchronous).

Educational Technology (Ed Tech): A field or practice that is focused on using technologies (i.e., man-made tools and physical spaces) for the advancement of learning. Robinson, Molenda, and Rezabek (2011) further describe educational technology to include 'the study and ethical practice of facilitating learning and improving performance by creating, using, and managing appropriate technological processes and resources' (p. 15).

Face-to-Face (F2F): This mode of teaching is often thought of as a 'traditional' mode of teaching. It takes place 'in real life' and normally within the classroom or studio setting.

Flipped Classroom: This form of teaching provides the student with resource activities (e.g., videos, text readings, podcasts) that students are to complete PRIOR to a synchronous class or seminar time. Rather than having the core class content taught during class time, the student learns the content through the resource material which allows for class time to be spent in building upon the ideas addressed in the resource materials.

Learning Management System (LMS): Generally utilized in an online or blended course, a Learning Management System (LMS) is a web-based application that provides a variety of communication tools for secure student use. Examples of LMS include: Blackboard, Moodle, Desire2Learn (D2L) and WebCT.

Online Learning: A mode of teaching that consists of 80 per cent to 100 per cent of the learning experience taking place in the online environment and less than 20 per cent in a face-to-face teaching mode.

Online Music Pedagogy: The art and science of teaching the discipline of music using online learning.

Synchronous music courses: Online, weekly schedule classes that are often developed similarly in topic and weekly design as their face-to-face class counterparts. The synchronous, or live, portion of the class occurs via a live, video conference stream.

References

Adileh, M. (2012). Teaching music as a university elective course through e-learning. *Australian Journal of Music Education, 1*, 71–9.

Alam, A. (2020). Challenges and possibilities of online education during Covid-19. *Preprints*, 2020060013. https://dx.doi.org/10.20944/preprints202006.0013.v1.

Alberich-Artal, E., & Sangra, A. (2012). European Journal of Open, Distance and E-Learning, n1. Virtual Virtuosos: A Case Study in Learning Music in Virtual Learning Environments in Spain.

Alcorn, A. A. (2018). One post and two responses: Enlivening the online discussion forum. *Pedagogy Development for Teaching Music Online* (pp. 263–85). Hershey, USA: IGI Global. https://dx.doi.org/10.4018/978-1-5225-5109-6.ch003.

Allen, E. I., & Seaman, J. (2004). *Entering the mainstream: The quality and extent of online education in the United States, 2003 and 2004.* Needham, MA: The Sloan Consortium, 2004.

Allen, E. I., & Seaman, J. (2013). *Changing course: Ten years of tracking online education in the United States.* Newburyport, MA 01950: Sloan Consortium. PO Box 1238.

Allen, E. I., & Seaman, J. (2014). Grade change: Tracking online education in the United States. *Babson Survey Research Group.* http://www.onlinelearningsurvey.com/reports/gradechange.pdf.

Allsup, R. E., & Benedict, C. (2008). The problems of band: An inquiry into the future of instrumental music education. *Philosophy of Music Education Review, 16*(2), 157–72.

Altowairiki, N. F. (2016). Inclusive online learning environment: Fundamental steps for universal design for learning incorporation in higher education. In *Proceedings of E-Learn: World Conference on E-Learning* (pp. 566–70). Washington, DC: United States: Association for the Advancement of Computing in Education (AACE). Retrieved 19 June 2021 from https://www.learntechlib.org/primary/p/173982/.

An, H., Shin, S., & Lim, K. (2009). The effects of different instructor facilitation approaches on students' interactions during asynchronous online discussions. *Computers & Education, 53*(3), 749–60. https://doi.org/10.1016/j.compedu.2009.04.015.

Anderson, L. W., Krathwohl, D. R., Airasian, P. W., Cruikshank, K. A., Mayer, R. E., Pintrich, P. R., Raths, J., & Wittrock, M. C. (Eds.) (2001). *A taxonomy for learning, teaching, and assessing: A revision of Bloom's taxonomy of educational objectives.* New York: Longman.

Arbaugh, J. B., Cleveland-Innes, M., Diaz, S. R., Garrison, D. R., Ice, P., Richardson, K., & Swan, K. P. (2008). Developing a community of inquiry instrument: Testing a measure of the community of inquiry framework using a multi-institutional sample. *The Internet and Higher Education*, *11*(3), 133–6. https://doi.org/10.1016/j.iheduc.2008.06.003.

Árnason, K., Arnason, A., & Briem, K. (2014). Playing-related musculoskeletal disorders among Icelandic music students. *Medical Problems of Performing Artists*, *29*(2), 74–9. https://doi.org/10.21091/mppa.2014.2017.

Arslan, G., Yıldırım, M., & Aytaç, M. (2020). Subjective vitality and loneliness explain how coronavirus anxiety increases rumination among college students. *DeathStudies*. https://doi.org/10.1080/07481187.2020.1824204.

Australian Curriculum, Assessment and Reporting Authority (ACARA). (n.d.). Website content. https://www.australiancurriculum.edu.au.

Baik, C., Larcombe, W., Wyn, J., Allen, L., Brett, M., Field, R., & Brooker, A. (2017). Stimulating curriculum and teaching innovations to support the mental well-being of university students. Final Report March 2017. *Report for the Australian Government, Department of Education and Training*. https://minerva-access.unimelb.edu.au/handle/11343/217777.

Bandura, A. (1981). Self-referent thought: A developmental analysis of self-efficacy. *Social Cognitive Development: Frontiers and Possible Futures*, 200(1), 239.

Bates, A. T. (2015). *Teaching in a digital age: Guidelines for designing teaching and learning*. BCcampus. https://openlibrary-repo.ecampusontario.ca/jspui/handle/123456789/276.

Bernard, C. F., Weiss, L., & Abeles, H. (2018). Space to share: Interactions among music teachers in an online community of practice. *Bulletin of the Council for Research in Music Education* Winter 2018 (215), 75–94. https://doi.org/10.5406/bulcouresmusedu.215.0075.

Bhatti, I., Jones, K., Richardson, L., Foreman, D., Lund, J., & Tierney, G. (2011). E-learning vs lecture: Which is the best approach to surgical teaching? *Colorectal Disease*, *13*(4), 459–62. https://doi.org/10.1111/j.1463-1318.2009.02173.x.

Biasutti, M., Antonini Philippe, R., & Schiavio, A. (2021). Assessing teachers' perspectives on giving music lessons remotely during the COVID-19 lockdown period. *Musicae Scientiae*. https://dx.doi.org/10.1177/1029864921996033.

Bigatel, P. M., Ragan, L. C., Kennan, S., May, J., & Redmond, B. F. (2012). The identification of competencies for online teaching success. *Journal of Asynchronous Learning Networks*, *16*(1), 59–78.

Biggs, J. B. (1987). Study process questionnaire manual. Student approaches to learning and studying. Australian Council for Educational Research Ltd., Radford House, Frederick St., Hawthorn 3122, Australia.

Biggs, J. (1999). What the student does: Teaching for enhanced learning. *Higher Education Research & Development*, *18*(1), 57–75. https://doi.org/10.1080/0729436990180105.

Biggs, J. (2003). Aligning teaching for constructing learning. *Higher Education Academy, 1*(4). https://www.heacademy.ac.uk/sites/default/files/resources/id477_aligning_teaching_for_constructing_learning.pdf.

Bjøntegaard, B. J. (2015). A combination of one-to-one teaching and small group teaching in higher music education in Norway – a good model for teaching? *British Journal of Music Education, 32*(1), 23–36. https://doi.org/10.1017/S026505171400014X

Black, P., & Wiliam, D. (1998). Assessment and classroom learning. *Assessment in Education, 5*(1), 7–75.

Borg, S. (2018). Evaluating the impact of professional development. *RELC Journal, 49*(2), 195–216. https://doi.org/10.1177/0033688218784371.

Borup, J., West, R. E., & Thomas, R. (2015). The impact of text versus video communication on instructor feedback in blended courses. *Educational Technology Research and Development, 63*(2), 161–84. https://doi.org/10.1007/s11423-015-9367-8.

Bourne, J., Harris, D., & Mayadas, F. (2005). Online engineering education: Learning anywhere, anytime. *Journal of Engineering Education, 94*(1), 131–46

Bowen, W. G., Chingos, M. M., Lack, K. A., & Nygren, T. I. (2013) Online learning in higher education: Randomized trial compares hybrid learning to traditional course. *Education Next, 13*(2), 58+.

Bower, M., Dalgarno, B., Kennedy, G., Lee, M. J. W., & Kenney, J. (2015). Design and implementation factors in blended synchronous learning environments: Outcomes from a cross-case analysis. *Computers & Education, 86,* 1–17. https://doi.org/10.1016/j.compedu.2015.03.006.

Branch, R. M., & Kopcha, T. J. (2014). Instructional design models. In Michael Spector, M. David Merrill, Jeroen van Merrienboer & Marcy P. Driscoll (Eds.), *Handbook of research on educational communications and technology* (pp. 77–87). New York, NY: Springer.

Brändström, S., Wiklund, C., & Lundström, E. (2012). Developing distance music education in Arctic Scandinavia: electric guitar teaching and master classes. *Music Education Research, 14*(4), 448–56. doi:10.1080/14613808.2012.703173.

Brown, J. S., & Duguid, P. (1991). Organizational learning and communities-of-practice: Toward a unified view of working, learning, and innovation. *Organization Science, 2*(1), 40–57.

Cheshire, L. (2019). Inclusive education for persons with disabilities – Are we making progress?: Background paper prepared for the international forum on inclusion and equity in education – Every learner matters. 11–13 September 2019, Colombia, CA. https://unesdoc.unesco.org/ark:/48223/pf0000370386.

Chickering, A. W., & Ehrman, S. C. (1996). Implementing the seven principles: Technology as lever. *American Association for Higher Education Bulletin, 49*(2), 3–6.

Clark, R. C., & Mayer, R. E. (2003). *E-Learning and the science of instruction: Proven guidelines for consumers and designers of multimedia learning.* San Francisco, CA: Jossey-Bass.

Clark, R. C., & Mayer, R. E. (2008). Learning by viewing versus learning by doing: Evidence-based guidelines for principled learning environments. *Performance Improvement, 47*(9), 5–13.

Coats, S. (2006). Thinking as you play: Teaching piano in individual and group lessons. *Indiana University Press*. https://dx.doi.org/10.1017/S0265051707007449.

Cook, D.A., Levinson, A.J., Garside, S., Dupras, D.M., Erwin, P.J., & Montori, V.M. (2008). Internet-Based Learning in the health Professions: A meta-analysis. *JAMA, 300*(10), 1181–96. doi:10.1001/jama.300.10.1181.

Cox, G. (2006). Transforming research in music education history. In R. Colwell (Ed.), *MENC Handbook of research methodologies*, pp. 73–94. New York: Oxford University Press.

Colwell, R, Hewitt, M., & Fonder, M. (2017). *The teaching of instrumental music*. New York: Routledge. https://doi.org/10.4324/9781315619033.

Crawford, R. (2013). Evolving technologies require educational policy change: Music education for the 21st century. *Australasian Journal of Educational Technology, 29*(5), 717–34. Document15. https://doi.org/10.14742/ajet.268.

Creswell, J. W. (2012). *Educational research: Planning, conducting, and evaluating quantitative and qualitative research* (4th ed.). Boston, MA: Pearson.

Csikszentmihalyi, M. (1988). The flow experience and its significance for human psychology. In *Optimal experience* (pp. 15–35). Cambridge, UK: Cambridge University Press.

Csikszentmihalyi, M. (1990). *Flow: The psychology of optimal experience*. New York, NY: HarperPerennial.

Damon, M., & Rockinson-Szapkiw, A. J. (2018). Online and face-to-face voice instruction: Effects on pitch accuracy improvement in female voice majors. In C. Johnson & V. C. Lamothe (Eds.), *Pedagogy development for teaching online music* (pp. 21–44). Hershey, USA: IGI Global. https://doi.org/10.4018/978-1-5225-5109-6.ch002.

Daubney, A., & Fautley, M. (2020). Editorial research: Music education in a time of pandemic. *British Journal of Music Education, 37*(2), 107–14. doi:10.1017/S0265051720000133.

Delle Monache, S., Comanducci, L., Buccoli, M., Zanoni, M., Sarti, A., Pietrocola, E., Berbenni, F., & Cospito, G. (2019). A presence- and performance-driven framework to investigate interactive networked music learning scenarios. *Wireless Communications and Mobile Computing* (4–5), 1–20. https://doi.org/10.1155/2019/4593853.

Dewey, J. (1910). *How we think*. New York, NY: D.C. Heath & Co.

Dewey, J. (1938). *Experience & education*. New York, NY: Simon & Schuster.

Draper, P. (2008). Music two-point zero: Music, technology and digital independence. *Journal of Music, Technology and Education, 1*(2–3), 137–52. https://doi.org/10.1386/jmte.1.2and3.137_1.

Dweck, C. (2016). What having a 'growth mindset' actually means. *Harvard Business Review, 13*, 213–26.

Dweck, C. S. (2019). The choice to make a difference. *Perspectives on Psychological Science, 14*(1), 21–5.

Dye, K. (2007). Applied music in an online environment using desktop videoconferencing. (Doctoral dissertation) Available from ProQuest Dissertations and Theses database. (UMI No.3259242).

Eakes, K. (2009). *A comparison of a sociocultural and a chronological approach to music appreciation in face-to-face and online instructional formats* (Unpublished doctoral dissertation). Auburn University, United States. (Publication No. AAT 3365532)

Educause. (2018). A day in the online life of a student. https://www.educause.edu/ecar/research-publications/ecar-study-of-undergraduate-students-and-information-technology/2018/a-day-in-the-online-life-of-a-student.

Elliott, D. J. (1995). *Music matters a new philosophy of music education.* New York: Oxford University Press.

Eremenko, V., Morsi, A., Narang, J., Serra, X. (2020). Performance assessment technologies for the support of musical instrument learning. Paper presented at: *CSEDU 2020 The 12th International Conference on Computer Supported Education.* 2–4 May 2020.

Ericsson, K. A. (1997). Deliberate practice and the acquisition of expert performance: An overview. In H. Jørgensen & A. C. Lehmann (Eds.), *Does practice make perfect? Current theory and research on instrumental practice* (pp. 9–51). Oslo, Norway: Norges musikkhøgskole.

Flyvbjerg, B. (2006). Five misunderstandings about case-study research. *Qualitative Inquiry, 12*(2), 219–45.

Forsyth, M., Tulk, J. E., & Turnbull, G. (2013). Notes from the field: Three perspectives on teaching music online. *Canadian Folk Music/Musique Folklorique Canadienne, 46*(4), 23–6. http://www.canfolkmusic.ca/index.php/cfmb/article/viewFile/587/575.

Fredrickson, W. E., Moore, C., & Gavin, R. (2013). Attitudes of select music performance faculty toward students teaching private lessons after graduation: A USA pilot study. *International Journal of Music Education, 31*(3), 331–45.

Gagné, R., & Driscoll, M. (1988). *Essentials of learning for instruction* (2nd ed.). Englewood Cliffs, NJ: Prentice-Hall.

Garrison, D. R. (2011). *e-Learning in the 21st-century: A framework for research and practice.* New York, NY: Routledge.

Garrison, D. R., Anderson, T., & Archer, W. (2001). Critical thinking, cognitive presence, and computer conferencing in distance education. *American Journal of Distance Education, 15*(1), 7–23. doi:10.1080/08923640109527071.

Gaunt, H. (2007). One-to-one tuition in a conservatoire: The perceptions of instrumental and vocal teachers. *Psychology of Music, 36*(2), 215–45. https://doi.org/10.1177/0305735607080827.

Gaunt, H. (2010). One-to-one tuition in a conservatoire: The perceptions of instrumental and vocal students. *Psychology of Music, 38*(2), 178–208. https://doi.org/10.1177/0305735609339467.

Groulx, T., & Hernly, P. (2010). Online Master's degrees in music education: The growing pains of a tool to reach a larger community. *Update: Applications of Research in Music Education*, *28*(2), 60–70. https://doi.org/10.1177/8755123310361765.

Gunawardena, C. N., & McIsaac, M. S. (2004). Distance education. In D. H. Jonassen (Ed.), *Handbook of research in educational communications and technology* (2nd ed., pp. 355–95). Mahwah, NJ: Lawrence Erlbaum Associates.

Habe, K., Biasutti, M., & Kajtna, T. (2021). Wellbeing and flow in sports and music students during the COVID-19 pandemic. *Thinking Skills and Creativity*, *39*, 100798. https://doi.org/10.1016/j.tsc.2021.100798.

Hallam, S. (1998). *Instrumental teaching: A practical guide to better teaching and learning*. Oxford: Heinemann Educational. https://doi.org/10.1017/S0265051799230276.

Hammond, M. (2005). A review of recent papers on online discussion in teaching and learning in higher education. *Journal of Asynchronous Learning Networks*, *9*(3). https://dx.doi.org/10.24059/olj.v913.1782.

Harasim, L. (2000). Shift happens: Online education as a new paradigm in learning. *The Internet and Higher Education*, *3*(1–2), 41–61. doi:10.1016/S1096-7516(00)00032-4.

Hattie, J. (2012). *Visible learning for teachers: Maximizing impact on learning*. London, UK: Routledge.

Hattie, J., & Timperley, H. (2007). The power of feedback. *Review of Educational Research*, *77*(1), 81–112. https://doi.org/10.3102/003465430298487.

Hebert, D. G. (2007). Five challenges and solutions in online music teacher education. *Research and Issues in Music Education*, *5*(1), 1–10.

Henderson, M., & Phillips, M. (2015). Video-based feedback on student assessment: Scarily personal. *Australasian Journal of Educational Technology*, *31*(1). https://doi.org/10.14742/ajet.1878.

Henriksen, D., Fanhoe, C., Mishra, P., & Deep-Play Research Group. (2014). Abstracting as a trans-disciplinary habit of mind. *TechTrends*, *58*(6), 3–7. https://doi.org/10.1007/s11528-014-0794-x.

Hewitt, A. (2009). Musical styles as communities of practice challenges for learning, teaching and assessment of music in higher education. *Arts and Humanities in Higher Education*, *8*, 329–37. https://doi.org/10.1177/1474022209339956.

Hill, C., & Lawton, W. (2018). Universities, the digital divide and global inequality. *Journal of Higher Education Policy and Management*, *40*(6), 598–610.

Hossain, M. S., Islam, M. S., Glinsky, J. V., Lowe, R., Lowe, T., & Harvey, L. A. (2015). A massive open online course (MOOC) can be used to teach physiotherapy students about spinal cord injuries: A randomised trial. *Journal of Physiotherapy*, *61*(1), 21–7. https://doi.org/0.1016/j.jphys.2014.09.008.

Hyland, F., & Hyland, K. (2001). Sugaring the pill: Praise and criticism in written feedback. *Journal of Second Language Writing*, *10*(3), 185–212. https://doi.org/10.1016/S1060-3743(01)00038-8.

Hyon-Won, L. (2011). Telepresence inspires new cross-border music-making. *The Korean Times*. Posted: 27 September 2011. https://www.koreatimes.co.kr/www/culture/2019/11/145_95539.html.

Ice, P., Curtis, R., Phillips, P., & Wells, J. (2007). Using asynchronous audio feedback to enhance teaching presence and students' sense of community. *Journal of Asynchronous Learning Networks*, *11*(2), 3–25.

Ilari, B. (2010). A community of practice in music teacher training: The case of Musicalização Infantil. *Research Studies in Music Education*, *32*(1), 43–60. https://doi.org/10.1177/1321103X10370096.

Johnson, C., & Cheok, T. (forthcoming). *Australia's tertiary online music landscape in 2020: A historical study*.

Johnson, C. (2017). Teaching music online: Changing pedagogical approach when moving to the online environment. *London Review of Education*, *15*(3), 439–56. https://dx.doi.org/10.18546/LRE.15.3.08.

Johnson, C. (2018). Online curriculum mapping: Designing for teaching presence in online music courses. In *Proceedings of E-Learn: World Conference on E-Learning in Corporate, Government, Healthcare, and Higher Education* (pp. 1425–31). Las Vegas, NV, United States: Association for the Advancement of Computing in Education (AACE). https://www.learntechlib.org/primary/p/185110/.

Johnson, C. (2018). Preparing for change: Getting ready for offering online music courses. In C. Johnson & V. C. Lamothe (Eds.), *Pedagogy development for teaching music online*. IGI Publications. https://doi.org/10.4018/978-1-5225-5109-6.ch001.

Johnson, C. (2020). A conceptual model for teaching music online. *Int'l Jrl on Innovations in Online Education*, *4*(2), 1–23. doi:10.1615/IntJInnovOnlineEdu.2020035128.

Johnson, C. (2021). A historical study (2007–2015) on the adoption of online music courses in the United States. *Int'l J on Innovations in Online Education*, *5*(1), 1–20. https://doi.org/10.1615/IntJInnovOnlineEdu.2021037316.

Johnson, C. & Altowairiki, N. (2017). Developing teaching presence in online learning through shared stakeholder responsibility. In P. Vu, S. Fredrickson & C. Moore (Eds.), *Handbook of research on innovative pedagogies and technologies for online learning in higher education* (pp. 151–77). Hershey, USA: IGI Global. doi:10.4018/978-1-5225-1851-8.ch08.

Johnson, C., & Cooper, T. (2013). Online professional development: Three approaches for engaging faculty through a constructivist framework. In R. McBride & M. Searson (Eds.), *In proceedings of society for information technology & teacher education international conference* (pp. 31–5). Washington, DC: United States: Association for the Advancement of Computing in Education (AACE). https://www.learntechlib.org/primary/p/48066/.

Johnson, C., & Hawley, S. (2017). Online music learning: Informal, formal and STEAM. *Int'll Jrl for Innov. in Online Ed*, *2*(1), 1–13. https://doi.org/10.1615/IntJInnovOnlineEdu.2017015989.

Johnson, C., Lamothe, V. C., Narita, F., Clark, I., Mulholland, J., & Meyers, N. (2018). Sharing our narratives on developing our practice in online music pedagogy. In C. Johnson & V. C. Lamothe (Eds.), *Pedagogy development for teaching music online* (pp. 218–35). Hershey, USA: IGI Global. https://doi.org/10.4018/978-1-5225-5109-6.ch012.

Johnson, C., & Lock, J. (2018). Making multimedia meaningful: Outcomes of student assessment in online learning. In E. Langran & J. Borup (Eds.), *Proceedings of society for information technology & teacher education international conference* (pp. 1542–9). Washington, DC: United States: Association for the Advancement of Computing in Education (AACE). https://academicexperts.org/conf/site/2018/papers/52476.

Johnson, C., McAlpine, K., & Merrick, B. (2019). MusicWorks: Supporting students' musical career paths through technology-Enhanced authentic learning. In P. Hycy Bull & J. Keengswe (Eds.), *Handbook of Research on Innovative Digital Practices to Engage Learners* (pp. 315–33). Hershey, USA: IGI Global. doi:10.4018/978-1-5225-9438-3.ch016.

Johnson, C., & Merrick, B. (2020). Enabling music students' well-being through regular zoom cohort chats during dhe Covid-19 crises. In R. Ferdig, E Baumgartner, R. Harshorne, R. Kaplan-Rakowski, & C. Mouza (Eds.), *Teaching, technology and teacher education during the COVID-19 pandemic: Stories from the field* (pp. 261–4). Association for the Advancement of Computing in Education (AACE). https://www.learntechlib.org/p/216903/.

Johnson, T., Wisniewski, M., Kuhlemeyer, G., Isaacs, G., & Krykowski, J. (2012). Technology adoption in higher education: Overcoming anxiety through faculty bootcamp. *Journal of Asynchronous Learning Networks*, *16*(2), 63–72.

Jonassen, D. H. (1991). Evaluating Constructivistic Learning. *Educational Technology*, *31*(9), 28–33. http://www.jstor.org/stable/44401696.

Jonassen, D. H. (2013). First principles of learning. In J. M. Spector, B. B. Lockee, S. E. Smaldino, & M. C. Herring (Eds.), *Learning, problem-solving and mindtools: Essays in honor of David H. Jonassen* (pp. 287–97). New York, NY: Routledge.

Joseph, D., & Lennox, L. (2021). Twists, turns and thrills during COVID-19: Music teaching and practice in Australia. *Music Education Research*, *23*(2), 241–55, https://doi.org/10.1080/14613808.2021.1906852.

Kaufman, D. M. (1989). Third generation course design in distance education. In R. Sweet (Ed.), *Post-secondary distance education in Canada: Policies, practices and priorities*, pp. 61–78. Alberta: Athabasca University and Canadian Society for Studies in Education.

Keast, D. A. (2009). A constructivist application for online learning in music. *Research & Issues in Music Education*, *7*(1), 8. https://doi.org/10.1080/10632913.2015.1011815.

Keller, C. (2005). Virtual learning environments: Three implementation perspectives. *Learning, Media and Technology*, *30*(3), 299–311.

Kenny, A. (2016). *Communities of musical practice*. New York: Routledge.

Killingback, C., Ahmed, O., & Williams, J. (2019). 'It was all in your voice'-Tertiary student perceptions of alternative feedback modes (audio, video, podcast, and screencast): A qualitative literature review. *Nurse Education Today*, *72*, 32–9.

King, A., Prior, H., & Waddington-Jones, C. (2019). Connect resound: Using online technology to deliver music education to remote communities, *Journal of Music, Technology & Education, 12*(2), 201–17. https://doi.org/10.1386/jmte_00006_1.

Kirschner, P., Strijbos, J. W., Kreijns, K., & Beers, P. J. (2004). Designing electronic collaborative learning environments. *Educational Technology Research and Development, 52*(3), 47–66.

Klingenstein, B. G., & Hagen, S. L. (2013). A case study in online delivery: Boarding the bullet train to an online music degree. In J. Keengwe (Ed.), *Research perspectives and best practices in technology integration*, pp. 197–216. Hersey, PA: IGI Publications. https://doi.org/10.4018/978-1-4666-2988-2.ch011.

Koehler, M., & Mishra, P. (2009). What is technological pedagogical content knowledge (TPACK)? *Contemporary Issues in Technology and Teacher Education, 9*(1), 60–70.

Koh, K. (2017). Authentic assessment. *Oxford Research Encyclopedia of Education*. https://dx.doi.org/10.1093/acrefore/9780190264093.D13.22.

Koutsoupidou, T. (2014). Online distance learning and music training: Benefits, drawbacks and challenges. *Open Learning: The Journal of Open, Distance and e-Learning, 29*(3), 243–55. http://doi.org/10.1080/02680513.2015.1011112.

Kruse, N. B., Harlos, S. C., Callahan, R. M., & Herring, M. L. (2013). Skype music lessons in the academy: Intersections of music education, applied music and technology. *Journal of Music, Technology & Education, 6*(1), 43–60. https://doi.org/10.1386/jmte.6.1.43_1.

Lai, C., Wang, Q., & Lei, J. (2012). What factors predict undergraduate students' use of technology for learning? A case from Hong Kong. *Computers & Education, 59*(2), 569–79.

Lave, J., & Wenger, E. (1991). *Situated learning: Legitimate peripheral participation*. Cambridge, UK: Cambridge University Press.

Leonard, C. (2019). Inclusive education for persons with disabilities – Are we making progress?: Background paper prepared for the international forum on inclusion and equity in education – Every learner matters. 11–13 September, 2019, Colombia, CA. https://unesdoc.unesco.org/ark:/48223/pf0000370386.

Lierse, S. (2015). Developing fully online pre-service music and arts education courses [online]. *Victorian Journal of Music Education, 1*, 29–34. https://search.informit.com.au/documentSummary;dn=063518243244801;res=IELHSS.

Lisboa, T., Jonasson, P., & Johnson, C. (2022). Synchronous online learning, teaching and performance. In G. McPherson (Ed.), *Oxford handbook of music performance, Volume Two*, pp. 499–527. New York: Oxford. https://doi.org/10.1093/oxfordhb/9780190058869.001.0001.

Lock, J., & Johnson, C. (2017). Learning from transitioning to new technology that supports online and blended learning: A case study. *Journal of Interactive Learning Research, 28*(1), 49–64.

Macon, D. K. (2011). Student satisfaction with online courses versus traditional courses: A meta-analysis. Available from ProQuest Dissertations and Theses database. (UMI No. 858611481)

Mamlok, D. (2017). Active listening, music education, and society. In *Oxford Research Encyclopedia of Education*. http://doi.org/10.1093/acrefore/9780190264093.013.186.

Mark, M., & Gary, C. L. (2007). *A history of American music education*. Lanham, USA: Rowman & Littlefield Education.

Marriott, P., & Teoh, L. K. (2012). Using screencasts to enhance assessment feedback: Students' perceptions and preferences. *Accounting Education*, *21*(6), 583–98. https://doi.org/10.1080/09639284.2012.725637.

Martinak, L. (2012). Virtually stress free: Keeping online graduate management students healthy. *The Journal of Continuing Higher Education*, *60*, 165–74.

Maslow, A. H. (1943). A theory of human motivation. *Psychological Review*, *50*(4), 370–96.

Masum, H., Brooks, M., & Spence, J. (2005). MusicGrid: A case study in broadband video collaboration. *First Monday*, *10*(5). https://doi.org/10.5210/fm.v10i5.1238.

Mayadas, A. F., Bourne, J., & Bacsich, P. (2009). Online education today. *Science*, *323*(5910), 85–9.

Mayer, R. E. (2014). Multimedia instruction. In J. M. Spector, M. D. Merrill, J. van Merrienboer, & M. P Driscoll (Eds.), *Handbook of research on educational communications and technology* (pp. 385–99). New York: Springer.

Mayer, R. E. (2019). How multimedia can improve learning and instruction. In J. Dunlosky, & K. A. Rawson (Eds.), *The Cambridge handbook of cognition and education* (p. 460–79). Cambridge University Press. https://doi.org/10.1017/9781108235631.019.

Mayer, R. E., & Moreno, R. (2003). Nine ways to reduce cognitive load in multimedia learning. *Educational Psychologist*, *38*(1), 43–52.

McAlpine, K. (2020). Etudiants sans frontiers: Facilitating online international cultural exchanges through music technology. *International Journal on Innovations in Online Education*, *4*(3), 1–16. https://doi.org/10.1615/IntJInnovOnlineEdu.2020035156.

McPherson, G. E., & Zimmerman, B. J. (2011). Self-regulation of musical learning: A social cognitive perspective on developing performance skills. In R. Colwell & P. Webster (Eds.), *MENC handbook of research on music learning, Volume 2: Applications* (pp. 130–75). Oxford University Press. https://doi.org/10.1093/acprof:osobl/9780199754397.003.0004.

McPherson, G. (2022). Self-regulated learning music microanalysis. In G. McPherson (Ed.), *Oxford handbook of music performance*, Volume One, pp. 553–575. New York: Oxford Press. https://doi.org/10.1093/oxfordhb/9780190056285.001.0001

McSwiggan, L. C., & Campbell, M. (2017). Can podcasts for assessment guidance and feedback promote self-efficacy among undergraduate nursing students? A qualitative study. *Nurse Education Today*, *49*, 115–21. https://doi.org/10.1016/j.nedt.2016.11.021.

McTighe, J., & Wiggins, G. (2012). *Understanding by design framework*. Alexandria, VA: Association for Supervision and Curriculum Development.

Means, B., Toyama, Y., Murphy, R., Bakia, M., & Jones, K. (2010). Evaluation of evidence-based practices in online learning: A meta-analysis and review of online learning studies. Report by U.S. Department of Education, Office of Planning,

Evaluation, and Policy Development: Policy and Program Studies Service. Retrieved from. www.ed.gov/about/offices/list/opepd/ppss/reports.html.

Meinz, E. J., & Hambrick, D. Z. (2010). Deliberate practice is necessary but not sufficient to explain individual differences in piano sight-reading skill: The role of working memory capacity. *Psychological Science, 21*, 914–19. https://doi.org/10.1177/0956797610373933.

Merck, K. A., & Johnson, R. M. (2017). Music education for students with disabilities: A guide for teachers, parents, and students. *The Corinthian, 18*(6). https://www.semanticscholar.org/paper/Music-Education-for-Students-with-Disabilities%3A-A-Merck-Johnson/f423b70fb1b48d18009621602607f78069b5b3f4.

Merriam, S. (1988). *Qualitative research: A guide to design and implementation*. San Francisco, CA: Jossey-Bass.

Merrill, M. D. (2002). First principles of instruction. *Educational Technology Research and Development, 50*(3), 43–59. doi:10.2307/30220335.

Merrick, B., & Johnson, C. (2020). Teaching music online in higher education: 2020 conference report. *Journal of Music, Technology and Education, 13*(1), pp. 95–108. https://doi.org/10.1386/jmte_00018_1.

Meyer, A., Rose, D.H., & Gordon, D. (2014). *Universal design for learning: Theory and practice*. Wakefield, MA: CAST.

Miles, M. B., Huberman, A. M., & Saldaña, J. (2014). *Qualitative data analysis: A methods sourcebook* (3rd ed.). Thousand Oaks, CA: Sage Publications.

Mitchell, A. (2020a). A professional development program to facilitate group music performance teaching. In J. Encarnacao & D. Blom (Eds.), *Teaching and evaluating music performance at university: Beyond the conservatory model*, pp.101–115. London, UK: Routledge.

Mitchell, A. (2020b). Implementing group teaching in music performance. In J. Encarnacao & D. Blom (Eds.), *Teaching and evaluating music performance at university* (pp. 119–31). London, UK: Routledge.

Molenda, M. (2015). In search of the elusive ADDIE Model. *Performance Improvement, 54*(2), 40–2. http://doi.org/10.1002/pfi.21461.

Moore, M., & Kearsley, G. (2011). *Distance education: A systemative view of online learning*. 3rd ed. Belmont, CA: Wadsworth.

Murat, Yıldırım, & Solmaz, Fatma (2020). COVID-19 burnout, COVID-19 stress and resilience: Initial psychometric properties of COVID-19 burnout scale. *Death Studies*. doi:10.1080/07481187.2020.1818885.

Nielsen, S. G. (2004). Strategies and self-efficacy beliefs in instrumental and vocal individual practice: A study of students in higher education. *Psychology of Music, 32*(4), 418–31. doi:10.1177/0305735604046099.

Noetel, M., Griffith, S., Delaney, O., Harris, N. R., Sanders, T., Parker, P., del Pozo Cruz, B., & Lonsdale, C. (2021). Multimedia design for learning: An overview of reviews with Meta-Meta-Analysis. *Review of Educational Research*. https://doi.org/10.3102/00346543211052329.

Oliveira-Torres, F. (2012). Pedagogia musical online: um estudo de caso no ensino superior de música a distância. Thesis Dissertation. http://hdl.handle.net/10183/61146.

Park, J. Y., & Bonk, C. J. (2007). Is online life a Breeze? A case study for promoting synchronous learning in a blended graduate course. *MERLOT Journal of Online Learning and Teaching*, 3(3), 1–14.

Pellegrino, K., Kastner, J. D., Reese, J., & Russell, H. A. (2018). Examining the long-term impact of participating in a professional development community of music teacher educators in the USA: An anchor through turbulent transitions. *International Journal of Music Education*, 36(2), 145–59.

Perkins, R., Reid, H., Araújo, L. S., Clark, T., & Williamon, A. (2017). Perceived enablers and barriers to optimal health among music students: A qualitative study in the music conservatoire setting. *Frontiers in Psychology*, 8, 968. https://doi.org/10.3389/fpsyg.2017.00968.

Perrin, A., & Jiang, J. (2018, March 26). *About three-in-ten U.S. adults say they are 'almost constantly' online.* Pew Research Center. https://www.pewresearch.org/fact-tank/2021/03/26/about-three-in-ten-u-s-adults-say-they-are-almost-constantly-online/.

Perves, R. (2012). Technology and the educator. In G. McPherson and G. Welch (Eds.), The Oxford Handbook of Music Education, Vol. 2. New York: Oxford University Press, pp. 457–475.

Peters, G. D. (1992). Music software and emerging technology: G. David Peters outlines the history of music software and hardware and explores the new developments and benefits of the emerging software for use in the classroom. *Music Educators Journal*, 79(3), 22–63.

Picciano, A. G. (2002). Beyond student perceptions: Issues of interaction, presence, and performance in an online course. *Journal of Asynchronous Learning Networks*, 6(1), 21–40. https://dx.doi.org/10.24059/olj.v6i1.1870.

Picciano, A. G. (2006). Online learning: Implications for higher education pedagogy and policy. *Journal of Thought*, 41(1), 75–94.

Pike, P. D. (2017). Improving music teaching and learning through online service: A case study of a synchronous online teaching internship. *International Journal of Music Education*, 35(1), 107–17. https://doi.org/10.1177/0255761415613534.

Plato. (1970) *The Republic.* B. Jowett (Trans.). New York, NY: Vintage Classics.

Polit, D. F., & Beck, C. T. (2010). Generalization in quantitative and qualitative research: Myths and strategies. *International Journal of Nursing Studies*, 47(1), 1451–8.

Power, M. (2008). The emergence of blended online learning. Journal of Learning & Teaching, 4(4). Retrieved from https://jolt.merlot.org/vol4no4/power_1208.htm.

Quinton, S., & Smallbone, T. (2010). Feeding forward: Using feedback to promote student reflection and learning – A teaching model. *Innovations in Education and Teaching International*, 47(1), 125–35. https://doi.org/10.1080/14703290903525911.

Rapanta, C., Botturi, L., Goodyear, P., Guardia, L., & Koole, M. (2020). Online university teaching during and after the Covid-19 crisis: Refocusing teacher presence and learning activity. *Postdigital Science and Education*, *2*(3), 923–94. https://doi.org/10.1007/s42438-020-00155-y.

Redmond, P. (2011). From face-to-face teaching to online teaching: Pedagogical transitions. In *Proceedings ASCILITE 2011: 28th annual conference of the Australasian Society for Computers in Learning in Tertiary Education: Changing demands, changing directions* (pp. 1050–60). Towoomba, Australia: Australasian Society for Computers in Learning in Tertiary Education (ASCILITE).

Reigeluth, C. M. (Ed.). (1999). *Instructional design theories and models: A new paradigm of instructional theory* (Vol. II). Mahwah, NJ: Lawrence Erlbaum Associates.

Ritchie, L., & Sharpe, B.T. (2021). Music student's approach to the forced use of remote performance assessments. *Frontiers in Psychology*, *12*(641667), 1–9. https://doi.org/10.3389/fpsyg.2021.641667.

Rogers, E. M. (2003). *Diffusion of innovations* (5th ed.). New York: Free Press.

Root-Bernstein, R. S., & Root-Bernstein, M. M. (1999). *Sparks of genius: The thirteen thinking tools of the world's most creative people.* New York: Houghton Mifflin.

Root-Bernstein, R. S., & Root-Bernstein, M. (2001). *Sparks of genius: The thirteen thinking tools of the world's most creative people.* New York: Houghton Mifflin Harcourt.

Rose, D., & Meyer, A. (2002). *Teaching every student in the digital age: Universal design for learning.* Alexandria, VA: Association for Supervision & Curriculum Development. https://doi.org/10.1007/s11423-007-9056-3.

Ruippo, M. (2003). Music education online. *Sibelius Academy*, *2*, 1–8.

Ruippo, M. (1999). Music education steps out of the classroom. *Musiikkikasvatus – Finnish Journal of Music Education*, *4*(1), 107–11.

Ruthmann, S. A. (2007). Strategies for supporting music learning through online collaborative technologies. In J. Finney & P. Burnard (Eds.), *Music education and technology: Education and digital technology* (pp. 131–41). London: Bloomsbury.

Salavuo, M. (2006). Open and informal online communities as forums of collaborative musical activities and learning. *British Journal of Music Education*, *23*, 253–71.

Schiavio, A., Biasutti, M., & Antonini Philippe, R. (2021). Creative pedagogies in the time of pandemic: A case study with conservatory students. *Music Education Research*, *23*(2), 167–78. https://doi.org/10.1080/14613808.2021.1881054.

Schön, D. A. (1983). *The reflective practitioner: How professionals think in action.* New York, NY: Basic Books Inc.

Schönwetter, D. J., Reynolds, P. A., Eaton, K. A., & De Vries, J. (2010). Online learning in dentistry: An overview of the future direction for dental education. *Journal of Oral Rehabilitation*, *37*(12), 927–40. https://doi.org/10.1111/j.1365-2842.2010.02122.x.

Scott, S. (2006). A constructivist view of music education: Perspectives for deep learning. *General Music Today*, *19*(2), 17–21. https://doi.org/10.1177/10483713060190020105.

Seamon, M. (2004). Short- and Long-Term differences in instructional effectiveness between intensive and semester-length courses. *Teachers College Record, 106*(4), 635–50. https://www.tcrecord.org.

Seaman, J., Allen, I. E., & Seaman, J. (2018). *Grade increase, tracking distance education in the United States*. Babson Park, MA: Babson Survey Research Group. https://onlinelearningsurvey.com/reports/gradeincrease.pdf.

Senge, P. M. (2006). *The fifth discipline: The art & practice of the learning organization* (REV). New York: Random House.

Spahn, C., Strukely, S., & Lehmann, A. (2004). Health conditions, attitudes toward study, and attitudes toward health at the beginning of university study: Music students in comparison with other student populations. *Medical Problems of Performing Artists, 19*(1), 26–34. https://dx.doi.org/10.21091/mppa.2004.1005.

Spector, J. M. (2001). An overview of progress and problems in educational technology. *Interactive Educational Multimedia* (3), 27–37.

Stevens, R. S., McPherson, G. E., & Moore, G. A. (2019). Overcoming the 'tyranny of distance' in instrumental music tuition in Australia: The iMCM project. *Journal of Music, Technology & Education, 12*(1), 25–47. https://doi.org/10.1386/jmte.12.1.25_1.

Tallent-Runnels, M. K., Thomas, J. A., Lan, W. Y., Cooper, S., Ahern, T. C., Shaw, S. M., & Liu, X. (2006). Teaching courses online: A review of the research. *Review of Educational Research, 76*(1), 93–135.

Tomlinson, Carol Ann. (2014). *The differentiated classroom: Responding to the needs of all learners*. Alexandria, VA: ASCD.

Vonderwell, S. (2003). An examination of asynchronous communication experiences and perspectives of students in an online course: A case study. *The Internet & Higher Education, 6*(1), 77–90. https://doi.org/10.1016/S1096-7516(02)00164-1.

Vygotsky, L. S. (1978). *Mind in society: The development of higher psychological processes*. Cambridge, MA: Harvard University Press. https://doi.org/10.2307/j.ctvjf9vz4.

Waddell, G., & Williamon, A. (2019). Technology use and attitudes in music learning. *Frontiers in ICT, 6*(11), 1–14. https://doi.org/10.3389/fict.2019.00011

Waldron, J. (2009). Exploring a virtual music community of practice: Informal music learning on the Internet. *Journal of Music, Technology & Education, 2*(2–3), 97–112. http://dx.doi.org/10.1386/jmte.2.2-3.97_1.

Waldron, J. (2018). Online music communities and social media. In *The oxford handbook of community music* (p. 109). Oxford University Press. https://doi.org/10.1093/oxfordhb/9780190219505.013.34.

Wang, F., & Hannafin, M. J. (2005). Design-based research and technology-enhanced learning environments. *Educational Technology Research and Development, 53*(4), 5–23.

Webster, P. (2007). Computer-based technology and music teaching in learning: 2000–2005. In L. Bresler (Ed.), *International handbook of research in arts education* (pp. 1311–28). Dordrecht: Springer.

Webster, P. (2011). Key research in music technology and music teaching and learning. *Journal of Music, Technology & Education, 4*(3). https://doi.org/10.1386/jmte.4.2-3.115_1.

Wenger, E. (1998). *Communities of practice: Learning, meaning, and identity.* Cambridge: Cambridge University Press. https://doi:10.1017/CBO9780511803932.

Wenger, E. (1998). Communities of practice: Learning as a social system. *Systems Thinker, 9*(5), 2–3. https://doi.org/10.1177/135050840072002.

Wenger, E., & Wenger-Trayner, B. (2015). Communities of practice: A brief introduction. Webpage. https://wenger-trayner.com/introduction-to-communities-of-practice/.

Wiggins, G., & McTighe, J. (2005). *Understanding by design* (2nd ed.). Boston, MA: Pearson.

Wiggins, G., Wiggins, G. P., & McTighe, J. (2005). *Understanding by design.* Alexandria, VA: ASCD.

Winne, P. H., & Butler, D. L. (1994). Student cognition in learning from teaching. In T. Husen & T. Postlewaite (Eds.), *International encyclopaedia of education* (2nd ed., pp. 5738–45). Oxford, England: Pergamon.

Winzer, M. (1992). *Educational psychology in the Canadian classroom.* (2nd ed.). Scarborough, ON: Ally & Bacon Canada.

Wright, G. B. (2011). Student-centered learning in higher education. *International Journal of Teaching and Learning in Higher Education, 23*(1), 92–7.

Yıldırım, M., & Solmaz, F. (2020). COVID-19 burnout, COVID-19 stress and resilience: Initial psychometric properties of COVID-19 burnout scale. *Death Studies.* https://doi.org/10.1080/07481187.2020.1818885.

Yin, R. K. (2014). *Case study research: Design and methods* (5th ed.). Los Angeles, CA: Sage.

You, J. W., & Kang, M. (2014). The role of academic emotions in the relationship between perceived academic control and self-regulated learning in online learning. *Computers & Education, 77,* 125–33. https://doi.org/10.1016/j.compedu.2014.04.018.

Zimmerman, B. J. (2011). Barry Zimmerman discusses self-regulated learning processes. *Emerging Research Fronts Commentary,* December 2011 – see http://archive.sciencewatch.com/dr/erf/2011/11decerf/11decerfZimm/.

Zimmerman, B. J. (2011). Motivational sources and outcomes of self-regulated learning and performance. In B. J. Zimmerman & D. H. Schunk (Eds.), *Handbook for self-regulation of learning and performance* (pp. 49–64). New York, NY: Routledge.

Index

accessibility 8–9, 21–2, 27–8, 69–71, 73, 77, 80, 84, 94, 104, 173
active learning 17–18, 130, 144
active listening 124
active participation 76, 114, 130, 154
ADDIE (analysis, design, develop, implement, and evaluation) model 61
Allen, J. 6, 19–20
Artificial Intelligence (AI) 166
assessment 28–9, 31, 59–61, 87, 108, 119, 133, 152
   academic integrity 114
   activities 103–4
   alternate 104–5
   authenticity in 87–92, 95, 128
   case studies 107–16
   components of 87–92
   design 92–5, 108, 112–14
   discussion activities 115
   feedback in 96–103, 111–13, 115–16
   formative 31, 92–4, 96–8, 102
   individual and group 95–6, 107, 110–11
   listening activities 115
   multiple 90, 109, 136
   online music 59, 87–9, 100, 105, 107–8, 147, 152, 164–5
   personal implementation 105
   planning 93–4
   realistic 87
   self-assessment (*See* self-assessment)
   summative 31, 92–3, 96
   technology in 109
asynchronous learning 8–9, 30, 42, 47, 51, 53, 57, 78, 81–2, 94, 100, 102, 126–7, 135–6, 142, 148–50, 170. (*See also* synchronous learning)
   recording activity (using SoundTrap) 165
   set-up 137–8
Australia 22, 70, 159, 173–4

authentic/authenticity 2–3, 16, 71, 87–92, 101, 107, 109–10, 113, 120, 127–8, 163, 177
   in assessments 87–92, 95, 128
   pedagogical tool of 128
autonomy in learning 17, 42, 97, 107, 109

Bachelor of Music (BMus) programmes 7–8, 21–2, 25, 27, 107, 112
blended learning model 5–7, 15, 19–20, 102, 130

Canadian MusicGrid Project 174
case studies
   for assessment 107–16
   for communication 46–56
   for design 30, 74–85
   three phases of data collection 25–6
class objectives 93, 96, 149
communication 28–30, 33–5, 60, 77, 79, 102, 108, 113, 119, 139, 154, 159, 169
   case studies 46–56
   clarity 36–8, 46–7, 55, 144
   creating video communication 143–5
   email 34, 41, 47, 50
   personal implementation 44
   presence and community 38–40, 48–50, 53–5
   technology tools in 42–3, 48, 50–4, 56
   timing 40–1, 47–8, 55
   videos (*See* videos/video creation)
   virtual backgrounds 40
Community of Inquiry (COI) model 20, 26, 28, 61–2
   survey 62
Community of Practice (CoP) 68, 170–2
   elements of 171
   Wenger's Stages of Development 171–2
Connect ReSound project 7, 174
conservatoires 22, 31, 33, 59, 62–3, 87, 153, 160, 173–4

constructive alignment 92–3
constructivism theory 15–22, 28, 31, 120, 130. (*See also* social constructivism)
  constructivist learning design 58–9
  and online teaching 162
continuum of technology-based learning 19–20
correspondence classes. (*See* distance learning)
Covid-19 pandemic 8–9, 22–4, 33, 59, 105, 119–20, 122, 152
creativity 11–12, 22, 27, 34, 87, 89, 112–13, 122–3, 125
curriculum differentiation 42, 70, 152

deep learning 17, 90
design 28–30, 64
  assessment in learning 92–5, 108, 112–14
  case studies 74–85
  constructivist learning design 58–9
  course design 28, 30, 45, 55, 58, 60, 62, 66, 73–7, 80, 82–4, 109 (*See also* online music courses)
  framework for teaching music online 64
    accessibility 69–70, 73, 77, 80, 84, 94
    organization 64–7, 73, 75–6, 79–82
    planning 67–9, 73, 76–7, 80, 82–3
    well-being 70–3, 77–8, 80–1, 84
  personal implementation 72
  pre-course 74–5
Dewey, J., reflection in learning 15–16
digital technology 19. (*See also* technology (technology-enhanced learning))
distance learning 3–4, 174
diversity of learning/teaching approach 17, 19, 54, 74, 76, 152
dual-mode teaching 20, 46–9, 51, 74, 137–40
  set-up 138–40
  synchronous music activities in 164

educational technology 4, 17, 19, 25, 79
e-learning 19–20, 129

equity 8, 129, 140
Erasmus+ INTERMusic project 174

Facebook 49, 51, 160, 176. (*See also* Twitter; YouTube)
face-to-face (F2F) learning/teaching 4, 7–8, 10–11, 19–24, 28, 34, 46–7, 49–50, 54, 57, 63, 65, 68, 74–6, 83, 87, 107, 110, 120, 123, 128, 135–9, 152–3, 159, 164, 170, 173. (*See also* online music learning; online music teaching)
feedback mechanism 2, 28, 35–6, 41–3, 51, 90, 92–3, 151–2
  in assessment 96–103, 111–13, 115–16
  audio-based 165
  critical friend feedback 91, 98
  formal/informal 98
  Hattie's levels of feedback 99–100
  immediate 46, 102, 127
  individual self-assessment 104
  instructor feedback 90, 93, 96, 100–1, 104
  open feedback dialogue 97
  peer review 93–4, 112, 151
  self-regulated learning through 59–61
  student-to-student 104
  text-based 101
  thematic analyses 101
  video 35–6, 100–2, 165
  ways of receiving feedback 98–9
flexibility 8, 70, 77, 84, 94, 109, 114, 127, 132, 135, 148, 173
flipped classroom technique 78
formal learning (graded) 91. (*See also* informal learning (non-graded))
formative assessment 31, 92–4, 96–8, 102. (*See also* summative assessment)
Framework for Promoting Student Mental Well-being in Universities 63

Garrison, D. R. 19–20
Google 80
group lessons 68–9, 95–6. (*See also* one-to-one/individual lessons)

Hattie, J., levels of feedback 99–100
higher education 2–4, 6–7, 18, 20–4, 27, 42, 101, 119, 144, 159, 172–4

hologram technology 166
hybrid teaching 6, 7, 48, 74–5, 108, 110

in-class learning 45–7, 53, 63, 93, 127, 139–40, 148, 153. (*See also* out-of-class learning)
inclusive learning design 18, 21, 42, 70
informal learning (non-graded) 91, 93. (*See also* formal learning (graded))
instructional design model 6, 18–19, 21, 23–4, 57–8, 61–2, 136
    ADDIE 61
instructor self-assessment 31, 108
intended learning outcomes (ILOs) 92
interactive approach 45, 69, 74, 76–8, 81, 84, 138

Jonassen, D. H. 16–17, 58

Kaufman, D. M. 3
knowledge sharing 159–63, 170–1
Koh, K. 89, 128

latency 12, 52, 110, 140, 164
learning by design model 61, 76
learning management system (LMS) 37–8, 41–2, 46, 48, 50–1, 53, 55, 60, 66, 79, 81–2, 91, 120, 136, 138, 144, 148
    organization and design 141–3
learning theory 2, 6, 15–17, 57
live-streamed classes. (*See* online music learning; online music teaching)

machine learning 166
master-apprentice approach 71
mentor/mentorship 169
meta-cognition 28, 90, 96
Milan Conservatoire 'G Verdi' institution 174
Mitchell, A. 69, 95
multimedia 6, 8, 18, 37, 69, 74, 82, 100
musculoskeletal injuries in musicians 62, 153
music appreciation 119, 162
music education (online) 1–2, 4, 15, 21–7, 52, 79, 91, 119, 130, 167, 176–7
music history 136, 161

musicianship 2, 21, 43, 58, 96, 151, 155
music instructors 6–8, 16, 22–6, 33–9, 42–3, 45–56, 58, 60–1, 65–6, 73–4, 76–8, 81, 83–4, 87, 90, 96, 108, 160, 169
    feedback of 90, 93, 96, 100–1, 104
    self-assessment 108
    time management 78–9
musicology 81, 83
music performance learning 15, 35, 59, 63, 93, 164–5
    video/video feedback in 101–2

National Association of Schools of Music (NASM) 7, 70, 152
networked music performances 7, 12, 174

on-campus class 8–9, 20, 35, 46–9, 51, 66, 74–5, 82, 91, 100, 122, 164, 174
one-to-one/individual lessons 68–9, 78, 95–6. (*See also* group lessons)
online community 163
    challenges within 50
online composition pedagogy 161
online music courses 2, 21, 24, 27–8, 30, 38, 44–5, 47–8, 50, 57–8, 61–2, 65–6, 72–5, 81, 83–4, 114
    copyright compliance 145
    design 131–5
        adjustment 133–4
        create 132–3
        non-performance classes 134–5
        organizer 98
        performance classes 134
        plan 131–2
    organization in 65
online music learning 2–9, 15, 19–22, 27, 57, 63, 71, 73, 159, 174. *See also* face-to-face (F2F) learning/teaching; online music teaching
    assumptions 9–10, 31, 35
    environment 57, 62, 65, 74, 94, 123, 128
    innovators of 4–6, 79, 167
    misconceptions 9–12
    student practice rooms 151–4
    at tertiary level 70
online music pedagogy (OMP) 2, 15, 21–2, 24, 50, 83, 161
    professional development in 27

online music performance 22, 162–4, 177
 3D Music Performance 166
online music teaching 8–9, 15, 22–5, 33, 63, 68, 83, 119–20, 160, 164, 171–3. (*See also* online music learning)
 assessment (*See* assessment)
 asynchronous 135–8 (*See also* asynchronous learning)
 authenticity in 127–8 (*See also* authentic/authenticity)
 basic technology tools 149–50
 beliefs and values of teaching 3, 120, 122–4
 communication (*See* communication)
 design (*See* design)
 essentials for 21
 global research projects in 174–5
 institutional parameters 129–30
 personal implementation 130
 purpose of 1–3
 re-design 30
 researchers in 160–3
 re-use and re-purpose 143
 self-reflection in 124–6
 set-up 137–40
 specific area of 174–5
 successful 145
 synchronous 136–8 (*See also* synchronous learning)
 teaching philosophy 120–1
 timing and design 120, 126–7
 trust 39–40
online presence 39, 154–5, 163
online recording software 89
out-of-class learning 148–9. (*See also* in-class learning)

pedagogy 21, 74, 78, 83, 110, 120, 123, 147–8
 OMP (*See* online music pedagogy (OMP))
 pedagogical paradigm shift 11, 23, 33, 65, 125
personalization 114, 123, 143
Piaget, J. 16
post-secondary music education 22, 25, 27, 177. (*See also* tertiary music classes)

Power, M. 4–5
professional learning networks 175–6

quizzes, online 45–6, 82, 112, 126

researchers in teaching music online 160–3
research-informed teaching practices 2, 23, 26, 69, 160
resilience/resiliency 59, 170
Royal Danish Academy of Music (RDAM) 174
Ruippo, M. 149, 174

Schön, D. A. 124–5
Seaman, E. 6, 19–20
self-assessment 91, 164
 individual self-assessment feedback 104
 instructor 31, 108
self-directed learning 59, 128, 170
self-efficacy 59, 99
self-reflection 3, 21, 28, 90–1, 95–6, 120, 164, 169
self-regulation 17, 23, 28, 66, 91, 95–6, 99, 147–8, 151, 164
 learning through feedback 59–61
Sibelius Academy, Finland 174
social constructivism 16, 24, 26, 28, 31, 54, 121, 130, 176. (*See also* constructivism theory)
social inclusivity 22, 24
social media 160. (*See also specific companies*)
students
 addressing anxiety in 62–4
 assessment design 109
 health and well-being 59, 63–4, 70–1, 73, 77–8, 80–1, 84, 153, 173
 motivation for 9, 17, 19, 30, 36, 42, 45, 48, 60, 65, 68, 97, 107, 123
 online course cohesion 110
 online student practice rooms 151–4
 student care 66, 71, 147–8
 student-centred learning approach 6, 16–18
 student engagement 19, 30, 39, 45, 60–1, 76–8, 144, 154–5
studio performance lessons 66, 68

summative assessment 31, 92–3, 96. (*See also* formative assessment)
supportive learning approaches 42, 140, 147, 149
synchronous learning 7, 9, 11, 22, 30, 38–42, 47–8, 50–3, 56–7, 66, 75–6, 78, 81–2, 102, 126–7, 136–7, 148–9, 159, 166, 170. (*See also* asynchronous learning)
  activities in dual-mode teaching 164
  practical synchronous session backup plans 141
  set-up 138

Teaching Music in Higher Education conference 172
technology (technology-enhanced learning) 3–4, 7, 10–11, 15, 17–18, 21–2, 24, 28, 30, 33, 57, 65, 74, 76, 80–2, 87, 107–8, 112, 122, 127, 129, 137–8, 148, 152, 160, 170, 176–7
  in assessment 109
  bi-directional 3
  demand for computing technology 5
  to develop community 154–5
  educational 4, 17, 19, 25, 79
  hologram 166
  LMS 42
  mobile device technology 80
  mono-directional 3
  smart phone 5
  suggestions for resolving issues 141
  tools 160–1
    basic tools 149–50
    in communication 42–3, 48, 50–4, 56
    guides for choosing tools 148–9
  in university-level music teaching 159, 172–4
  video conferencing technology 6, 38, 42
  video editing software 34

tertiary music classes 18, 63, 70, 152, 159 (*See also* post-secondary music education)
text-based format 35, 61
time management 35, 47, 53, 65, 73, 78–9, 84
TPACK (Technological Pedagogical Content Knowledge) approach 28
traditional apprentice-style disciplines 173
trans-disciplinary skills 89–90
transformation 8, 59, 129
Trinity Laban Conservatoire 174
Twitter 45, 56, 160, 176. (*See also* Facebook; YouTube)

undergraduate teaching, elements for 18–19
The United States 6, 20, 22, 159, 173
  NASM-accredited universities in 7
Universal Design for Learning (UDL) 9, 18, 69–70, 79–80, 100, 152

videos/video creation 34–6, 38–40, 51
  assumptions 35–6
  creating video communications 143–5
  instructor video responses 103–4
  on-screen focus 144
  speaker position on screen 144–5
  video conferencing technology 6, 38, 42, 75, 81, 138–9, 151, 176
  video course map 66
  video editing software 34
  video feedback 35–6, 100–2, 165
  video journals 103–4, 150–1
  video recording (software) 35, 43, 49–50, 65, 90
  Zoom rooms 43, 151, 154

web camera 39–40, 46
Wenger, E., Stages of Development 171–2

YouTube 7, 53, 79–80, 126. (*See also* Facebook; Twitter)

www.ingramcontent.com/pod-product-compliance
Lightning Source LLC
Chambersburg PA
CBHW061827300426
44115CB00013B/2285